50 Strategies for Communicating and Working with Diverse Families

SECOND EDITION

JANET GONZALEZ-MENA

Beginning Together

PEARSON

Boston   Columbus   Indianapolis   New York   San Francisco   Upper Saddle River
Amsterdam   Cape Town   Dubai   London   Madrid   Milan   Munich   Paris   Montreal   Toronto
Delhi   Mexico City   Sao Paulo   Sydney   Hong Kong   Seoul   Singapore   Taipei   Tokyo

Vice President and Editor in Chief: Jeffery W. Johnston
Acquisitions Editor: Julie Peters
Editorial Assistant: Tiffany Bitzel
Vice President, Director of Marketing and Sales Strategies: Emily Williams Knight
Vice President, Director of Marketing: Quinn Perkson
Marketing Manager: Erica DeLuca
Marketing Coordinator: Brian Mounts
Project Manager: Susan Hannahs
Production Editor: Kerry J. Rubadue
Art Director: Jayne Conte
Cover Designer: Bruce Killmer
Cover Art: Tim Gonzalez-Mena
Full Service Agency/Composition: Swapnil K. Vaidya GGS Higher Education Resources/PMG Inc.
Printer/Binder: Courier/Kendallville
Cover Printer: Lehigh-Phoenix Color/Hagerstown
Text Font: Optima

Credits and acknowledgments borrowed from other sources and reproduced, with permission, in this textbook appear on appropriate page within text.

Every effort has been made to provide accurate and current Internet information in this book. However, the Internet and information posted on it are constantly changing, so it is inevitable that some of the Internet addresses listed in this textbook will change.

Library of Congress Cataloging-in-Publication Data

Gonzalez-Mena, Janet.
   50 strategies for communicating and working with diverse families /
Janet Gonzalez-Mena. — 2nd ed.
      p. cm.
   Rev. ed. of: 50 early childhood strategies for working and
communicating with diverse families. c2007.
   Includes bibliographical references and index.
   ISBN-13: 978-0-13-700231-3
   ISBN-10: 0-13-700231-9
   1. Children—Services for—United States.   2. Early childhood
education—United States.   3. Family services—United States.
4. Multiculturalism—United States.   I. Gonzalez-Mena, Janet. 50 early
childhood strategies for working and communicating with diverse
families.   II. Title.   III. Title: Fifty strategies for communicating
and working with diverse families.
   HV741.G637 2010
   362.70973—dc22
                                              2009027694

10 9 8 7 6 5 4 3 2 1

www.pearsonhighered.com

ISBN 10:   0-13-700231-9
ISBN 13: 978-0-13-700231-3

Introduction

This practical book provides strategies on partnering with families to support, enhance, and maximize the quality of care and education of young children. Many of the strategies in this book address ideas about how early childhood professionals can create a climate of trust by communicating with family members in a collaborative way. The goal is to create useful, inclusive programs that respect and honor differences in families and individuals. These easy-to-use strategies provide a strong basis for working and communicating productively with families of all types and from varied backgrounds.

NEW IN THIS EDITION

The second edition of this book looks quite different from the first! The strategies are now grouped in categories rather than arranged alphabetically. The old strategies have new names, and some have been combined to make room for additional strategies that did not appear in the first edition. Diversity is a theme throughout the book, but it shows up first and foremost in a brand new Section 1, on varying types of families and family composition. This edition puts more emphasis on kindergarten and primary-grade teachers using the strategies than the first edition did. This new emphasis shows up in examples and stories about teachers and families. Based on reviewers' feedback, new subjects include working with families to maintain home language, deciding about holidays in the classroom, addressing media issues, improving child nutrition, getting children outside in nature, and dealing with a death in the family.

FAMILY-CENTERED CARE AND EDUCATION

This book is based on the concept called *family-centered care and education*. The tendency in the early care and education field has been to focus on the child, and indeed, some programs actually use the words "child-centered programs" in their philosophy statements. This book is based on the idea that you can't separate the child from the context of the family. *The child* is a term that has no real meaning, because no child stands alone; the influences of the family are always present. When programs regard those influences as a good thing, they are on their way to becoming family-centered. When a program becomes family-centered, diversity is a part of the package. You'll see that respecting diversity is addressed in two major sections and is a highlight in many of the strategies. Where respecting diversity isn't highlighted, it is quietly implied. With diversity comes the idea of equity as well as inclusion, meaning that you have to include everybody. You can't celebrate diversity and then exclude some families from the program because they or their children are too *different*. This book is about including *all* families and their children. It's about honoring diversity, even when it is hard to do so.

WHAT DOES "PARTNERSHIP" REALLY MEAN?

Partnership is another theme in this book. In building partnerships, establishing trust is key, because you can't have a partnership without trust. A partnership is different from merely trying to get families to cooperate with the program and carry out its goals. Involving parents is an approach often taken with that idea in mind. Policymakers learn about how school readiness and academic achievement are strengthened when parents are involved in their children's education. They jump on a bandwagon to teach parents how to help their children carry out the program goals. The parents then learn how to help their children according to the school's way of doing things.

A partnership is different from that kind of parental involvement, because it implies equity and shared power rather than one side dominating the other. In a partnership, roles and responsibilities may differ, but both sides have rights. At the heart of the partnership lies the welfare of the child. Each partner—family member and teacher—brings different strengths and skills to the union. Partners collaborate rather than issue orders. In a partnership, communication is two way rather than hierarchical. It takes communication skills for two parties to work in partnership. Accordingly, many of the strategies in this book relate to communication. Communication may be very different if the focus of the school is merely about getting parents on board so that they can help their children by doing at home what the school system and educators see as beneficial to readiness or academic achievement.

TRANSFORMATIVE EDUCATION IS THE MODEL

An approach to involving parents is often linked with parental education. The partnership approach is not the same, even though both involvement and education may well be part of it. Certainly, families who are involved in a program are more likely to take their partnership role seriously. Also, early childhood education professionals have knowledge, experience, and expertise that parents can benefit from; at the same time, parents know their own children, goals, beliefs, values, family traditions, and culture better than anyone else. So the educational model here is *transformative education* rather than the traditional teacher-student, one-way educational approach.

Transformative education is defined as two people or groups coming together and interacting in such a way that both parties learn something and are changed for the better by the interaction.

SOLVING THE NAME DILEMMA

In writing this book, I was faced the problem of what to call the adults who work in early childhood programs. This book takes in a wide sweep of early childhood and includes children from birth to age 8. Although all adults in these programs could be called *teachers*, some who work with the youngest children resist that term, because they don't *teach*, they *care for*. Others who resist the term *teacher* think of themselves as facilitators of learning and prefer to call themselves as *educators*. Still other adults who work with children in that age range work out of their homes, not in schools or centers, and call themselves *family child care providers*. Early childhood education is a complex field, and no one name works for everybody in it.

I also had to figure out a name for the early childhood programs themselves that included all the different forms. A third-grade classroom with a teacher is different from an infant-toddler center with caregivers, yet both fit under a label *early childhood education*. A half-day preschool is different from a kindergarten and also from a full-day child care program, which is different from a hospital child care center that is open 24 hours a day to serve staff on all shifts.

CARE AND EDUCATION CAN NEVER BE SEPARATED

So what names did I use? I addressed the dilemma by changing "early childhood education" to "early care and education" and calling the adults who work in the field teachers at some times and *early care and education professionals* or early childhood professionals at other times. Adding the word *care* highlights the idea that care and education can never be separated in the early years. The letters ECE, which are commonly used to define the programs for children ages birth to age 8 are used by some to mean *Early Childhood Education*. I use those letters to mean *Early Care and Education* to broaden the scope. To me it is very important to link education with care and not use the term education alone even when the example is in a primary classroom in a public school.

For young children, care is always a part of the educational process. Nell Noddings writes about this subject in many books, and she takes in the whole realm of education when she says care must always be part of it—through higher education even. My point is that though you may separate programs by the age of the children they serve and give them different labels, all should include both education and care.

Other terms also varied by the focus of the strategy, so sometimes I used *school* and *classroom*, and other times I used *program* and *center*. Sometimes I was aiming more at teachers in school and other times more at staff in programs, such as prekindergarten or preschool, infant-toddler programs, early intervention programs, child care, Head Start, Early Head Start, and school-age child care. It's complex, because these programs take place in a variety of environments, including centers, schools, or homes, and some strategies pertain more to one setting than to the others.

In summary, this book is a targeted text that offers practical strategies for partnering with families, creating the trust necessary for true collaboration and developing programs that include all families and individuals. Of course, at the heart of all these useful strategies lies the welfare of the child.

ACKNOWLEDGMENTS

I would like to thank the following people for helping make this book what it is: Marion Cowee, Lynn Doherty, Tim Gonzalez-Mena, Lisa Lee, Kitty Ritz, Ethel Seiderman, and Joan Symonds. In addition, I wish to thank the following reviewers for their suggestions and insights: Irene Cook, California State University, Bakersfield; Sandi Jessen, Minnesota State University, Mankato; Alycia Maurer, University of Texas, San Antonio; and Lynda Roberts, Cerritos College.

Contents

APPRECIATING ALL KINDS OF FAMILIES

WHAT TEACHERS NEED TO KNOW

Families come in all kinds of sizes, shapes, structure, configurations, and makeup. For example, there are two-parent families, single-parent families, and extended families with several generations in one household. There are stepfamilies and blended families, biracial families, gay families, and straight families. Transnational families may live in two countries. Migrant families may move where the work is. Children may have been born into the family or come by other means, such as foster care, adoptions, or kinship networks. Some children live in more than one home and are members of more than one family.

There are many definitions of *family*. Those definitions may focus on genetics, residence, emotional ties, rules, or legal status. The American Academy of Family Physicians (2003) defines family as "a group of individuals with a continuing legal, genetic, and/or emotional relationship." One teacher defines family as "the people living in the children's homes who love and care for them," and this same teacher also makes sure that all families are welcomed and respected (Rieger, 2008). She lets children and their families know that if they care to, they can talk about family members who may not be with them, recognizing that military duty, divorce, incarceration, and death can separate family members from the child.

Not all families have homes. The general view of the homeless population may be of city-dwelling, single adult men with mental illness, alcohol, or drug additions, but the truth is that homeless families are everywhere and many of them have children. This group needs the same respect and consideration as any other group of families and often needs more support and services than most families in the school or other early childhood setting. Homelessness disrupts every aspect of family life including the health and wellbeing of the members and the education of their children (Thoennes, 2008).

In a workshop, Linda Brault (2007) asked participants to categorize their families in terms of size by raising their hands when she asked, "How many grew up in a large family? A small family? A medium-sized family." There was wide disparity in their concept of large, small, and medium families. Some counted only their parents and siblings. Others counted extended family members. When the presenter questioned individuals further, it became clear they had very different definitions of families and membership in them. For example, some counted dead people as family members and deemed them as important as live family members. For other participants, nonrelatives had the same status as blood relatives. This was a racially, ethnically, and culturally diverse group, which showed the many different concepts about who makes up a *family*.

One of the problems in working with diverse families arises when the teacher's notion of family gets in the way of understanding and respecting all kinds of families. The problem is magnified when a family who doesn't live up to the teacher's picture of an ideal family is suspected of child abuse while the same teacher overlooks signs of abuse in an "ideal" family. Since teachers and other early childhood professionals are mandated reporters, the repercussions could be serious, not only for the children and the families but also for the teacher.

While looking at all the different kinds of families who teachers and other early educators can work with, recent immigrants are in a special category. Immigrant status may have a huge influence on how the family operates. It's important to recognize that all Americans, except for the Native Americans, were once immigrants. It's also important to realize that at one time or another, most immigrant groups have been blamed for the woes of the nation. Some immigrant families face a good deal of prejudice in addition to the other challenges facing them as they settle in a country that is different from the one in which they were born. Early care and education programs—schools—should support these families and do what they can to help them deal with their many challenges.

WHAT TEACHERS CAN DO

- Start by putting aside the idea of a "normal" or "ideal" family. Broaden your definition of family. When you approach a family who doesn't fit your ideal, you see them as "other," and othering people gets in the way of getting to know them and building a relationship. For many, the ideal family consists of a mother, father, two children, and maybe a dog, who all live together enjoying a middle-class lifestyle. That's one kind of family—there are many others!

- Realize that families who don't fit common notions of normal or ideal have to deal with being stereotyped, discriminated against, or ignored. Even though research on stereotypes is increasing, much of it focuses on race, gender, and religion more than on changing the stigmas attached to families who vary from what is considered "the norm."

- Recognize that teachers must value all families and move away from stereotypes and preconceived ideas about different kinds of families.

- Examine your program and institution to shed light on how the curriculum, materials, administrative hiring practices, and policies teach children and parents lessons about values related to families. The goal should be for all families to receive the same respect.

- If you have family figures for a dollhouse or block area, put them all in one container, and let children decide for themselves how they want to configure a family. Don't set them up the way they came, with matching mother, father, and children.

- Learn to communicate and build relationships with people who are different from yourself, and become aware of the pitfalls of miscommunication.

- Be aware of the kinds of activities and assignments that relate to the child's family or the family's history, which may be painful, unavailable, or unknown. Asking about the origin of a child's name or for baby pictures can be a problem for children who were adopted past infancy. Asking a family to share artifacts can be painful if they fled from their homeland with only the clothes on their backs.

- Instead of celebrating Mother's Day or Father's day as such, create a celebration day for children to show their gratitude for the person or persons who care for them. Let them choose who that person or persons are. Mother's Day or Father's Day can be painful for some single-parent or gay and lesbian families.

- Use a variety of means for contacting, working with, and involving family members in their children's out-of-home education and care.

- Get families involved with each other, and create a community.

- Recognize that the teacher has a good deal to learn from families—teaching should be regarded as a two-way process, which can be called a teaching-learning process, where the teacher and the learner often trade places.

2 WORKING WITH IMMIGRANT FAMILIES

WHAT TEACHERS NEED TO KNOW

Newly arrived immigrant families have a good many challenges. A huge one can be language. At a time when new immigrants have so many new things to learn, their communication system may be compromised. All the change of leaving the old behind and starting new in a strange culture brings stress. Language difficulties greatly add to the stress. Nothing is easy, and immigrants meet up with intolerant people while they are getting settled—finding a place to live, signing up for utilities, understanding the transportation system, and getting a new job. When people can't understand them, they get impatient with the immigrants. In a new language and culture, immigrants are slower than in their old country. They make many mistakes and sometimes are regarded as ignorant; however, if you could see them operate in their own language and familiar surroundings, they aren't the same people!

At a time when they need support, many immigrants are on their own. They have had to leave their support networks, including the extended family, behind. Maybe for the first time in their lives, they are alone in the world.

After immigrants have been here awhile, the children in the family often get ahead of the adults in learning the language and figuring out the new ways of the society they live in. That situation puts parents at a huge disadvantage, because traditional roles are reversed. Now the children are the ones who know best. They may even be embarrassed by their parent's awkward ways and difficulties in communication, even their accents. Where once respect for the authority of elders was the rule, now the children are the authorities. What worries for a family! Discipline may no longer work, and the children, too, are on their own.

Even though families may be uncomfortable about what is happening to their children, they have to send them to school, which may be quite different from their own country. Sometimes they are forced to put their children in out-of-home care. Grandma is no longer there to stay with them, and immigrants may be unhappy about turning their children over to nonfamily members in child care programs. They may worry about identity issues and that their children may become assimilated and lose their cultural ties.

Although sometimes immigrant families disagree with what they see in the school or other early care and education program, they may feel as if they are putting their children into the hands of those they consider to be the authority, especially if such a person is called *teacher* or *director*. "The professional knows best" is their attitude. These families may have great respect for authority. Some families still see themselves as the authority at home; in their minds, they create a huge separation between what they do at home and what happens in the early childhood program. Other families grant the teacher or other early childhood education professional supreme authority over all things to do with children, both in the program and at home. They see their job is to learn about it so that they can do the same at home. When one teacher told a family who recently immigrated from another country they should speak English to their children at home, they followed her advice even though their ability to speak English was limited. The result was that parent-child communication was greatly limited, and everyone was frustrated for a long time. The parents' English improved, but they always had a heavy accent and never became truly articulate in that language as compared to their own. The children learned English from school and from their peers but, to their parents' great sorrow, lost their home language. (See Strategy 39, Maintaining Home Language.)

This sign was on the wall of a kindergarten classroom to make families feel welcome by finding their own language displayed.

Alicia Lieberman, a mental health specialist, offers strategies for working with immigrant families in her article "Concerns of Immigrant Families" (1995). The strategies she suggests include those listed below.

WHAT TEACHERS CAN DO

- If there is a language difference, remember to work with it. Talk as clearly as you can using short sentences and plain words. Avoid jargon.
- Explain the routine of the program or classroom. Families may come from countries where the customs are very different.
- Acknowledge tension, and think about the reasons for it. Chances are that the tension between you and the parent is due to cultural differences.
- Ask parents about their child-rearing practices. Find out how things are done in their country when you don't understand a particular behavior or practice. Try to communicate about your difference so that it's seen by the family as just that—a difference—and not as a deficiency on their part.
- Serve as a cultural bridge between the parents' culture and the culture of classroom or child care program. Help the parents understand the way things are done in the classroom or center
- Remember that you are an authority figure and that most families want your approval.
- Establish a trusting atmosphere that encourages dialogue. Build trust before you try discussing problems, and when you do, try to discuss them in ways that avoid a critical tone and, instead, express care and concern.
- Remember that immigration causes great stress for the whole family. People who felt self-confident and competent in their home country are now trying to learn some basic skills. They may be suffering from depression. But many immigrants with children in early care and education programs are full of hope for the future. You are part of that hope.
- Appreciate their culture, support them, and help them adjust to life in a new country.

Notice what is on the bulletin board under Broadway Children's School. How do you think immigrants feel when they find their own language in evidence around the classroom? That's one way of saying, "You are welcome here."

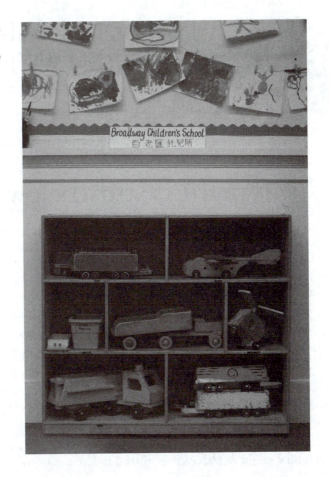

3 INCLUDING FAMILIES OF CHILDREN WITH SPECIAL NEEDS

WHAT TEACHERS NEED TO KNOW

Classrooms and centers set up for typically developing children are now required by law to accept children with special needs. All children must be provided with care and education in the least restrictive setting where their typically developing peers are served. That law has provided benefits to everybody—not just to the children and families with special needs. By making a program or school inclusive, everybody gains for the following reasons:

1. Diversity of all sorts is a bonus. Everybody benefits from being around people who are different from themselves—children and parents alike—especially if the early childhood professionals know how to help them appreciate differences and interact with each other in respectful ways.

2. Children with special needs benefit by being integrated with their typically developing peers instead of being segregated into special education programs. They learn to live in a world that has a greater variety of people in it than they would find in special education programs that are exclusively for them.

3. Teachers benefit by expanding their knowledge of how to meet a variety of needs, some of which they might not have encountered before they experienced inclusion.

4. Families who have children with special needs benefit from being integrated with families who have typically developing children and learning about them and their successes and challenges, just as those families with typically developing children benefit from learning about the successes and challenges of families of children with special needs.

WHAT TEACHERS CAN DO

- If parents of children who have special challenges or disabilities do not arrive in the classroom already acting as advocates for their children, encourage them to take on that role. (See Strategies 12 and 13 on advocacy.) They will need those skills as their children move on from your program or classroom to others. If they are already advocates, you need to appreciate that. You can learn a good deal from families and from the specialists with whom they are involved.
- Give emotional support to all families when needed. Recognize that families who have children with special needs or challenges may need even more support and understanding. Although many families have already had plenty of experience in coping with their emotions, others may be still at the stages of grieving that accompany the discovery that their child's development is not following a typical pathway. Feelings of anger, sadness, resentment, frustration, and guilt are common.
- Don't judge parents who are in denial or seem to be overprotective of their child. Accept them as they are, and realize that these are common responses for parents in their situation.
- Understand that some families have had multiple experiences working with professional experts and that their reactions to you may have nothing to do with you personally. If their experiences with other experts have been negative, it may take more time for you to build a relationship with

these parents than with parents who enter the program having little or no prior experience with experts.

- Be prepared to connect with specialists (if any) who are working with the family. Teamwork is important in meeting any child's needs, and including specialists and family members in the team may be helpful in meeting the special needs of some children. Parents may know more about their child's condition than you do, and the specialists working with them may have expertise that you can use.
- Use "people first" terminology. Don't say "a disabled child"; say "a child with a disability." Don't say "special-needs family"; say "a family who has a child with special needs."
- Provide opportunities for the both the child and the family members to integrate into the program or classroom. Introduce the family to other families, and help them to get to know each other.
- Learn about community resources (see Strategy 46) that are available to all families. The family who has a child with a disability or other challenges may be able to expand your knowledge of community resources based on their experience.
- The other strategies in this book that apply to parents in general can work equally well with parents of children having special needs.

A story about the benefits of parental involvement in an inclusion program: A mother brought her baby to a Mommy and Me class for the first time when he was 17 months old. Her child was born with a heart defect and had several surgeries in his young life. His main experience outside the home was with heart specialists and medical procedures. The nursery classroom was an entirely new experience for both him and his mother. His mother was shocked when she saw the skills that other children her son's age had developed. It was her first experience being around babies other than her own, and she had no idea of the developmental issues her child had been dealing with—issues that had been ignored in the interest of saving his life. She vowed from that day forward to focus more on his development and less on his medical problems, and she spoke right away to the specialists who had been seeing her son. They directed her to the resources she needed. She continued in the class, and everybody was delighted at the progress the boy made in a short time, once he got in an environment that was developmentally appropriate and conducive to his needs.

4 CREATING AN ANTIBIAS ENVIRONMENT

WHAT TEACHERS NEED TO KNOW

Although *antibias* is a word that some people find unnecessarily negative, it belongs to a particular tradition that those in early childhood education should know about. The term *pro-diversity* puts a positive spin on the word but doesn't connect it to the antibias movement in the same way. Many early childhood education professionals and parents first heard of the movement in the book *The Antibias Curriculum,* written by Louise Derman-Sparks and the Antibias Curriculum Task Force in 1987.

What is an antibias environment? Let's start with a typical early childhood environment before the antibias movement began. You could walk into almost any classroom or child care center and look around at what was on the walls, in the dramatic play area (often called "housekeeping corner" back then), in the book area, and in the refrigerator. You would find pictures, books, and puzzles representing families and children of European roots. Somewhere, you'd find "community helpers" who were white and also segregated by gender. The firefighters and police officers were all men, as were the doctors. The teachers, nurses, and librarians were all women. Although the food may have been

Part of an antibias approach is creating an environment that welcomes men as much as it welcomes women.

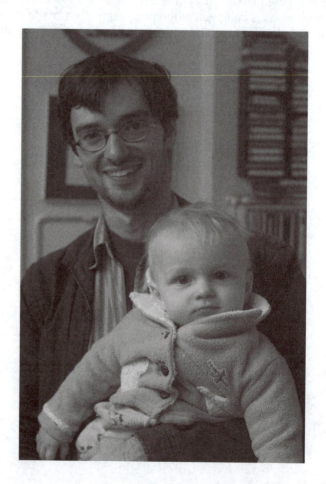

that of the area the classroom was in, it was food with which European Americans in that region were most familiar. Even if the staff was diverse, the environment didn't reflect this diversity or their backgrounds. Furthermore, it was obvious that the people in charge were from one group and the aides and cleaning people were from another. This isn't ancient history. You can still find this kind of situation in some classrooms and other early childhood education programs today, although there has been some change.

Now let's take a walk through an antibias environment. Pretend that you enter the door of a classroom or child care center. You look around and see pictures on the wall representing the diversity of the children and their families—and of the greater society. You notice that some pictures are of women in a variety of jobs and roles, as well as various pictures of men. When you walk over to the book area, you see that same diversity represented not only in the pictures and stories but also in the languages. Books are available in the various home languages of the children. Some are commercial, and some are homemade. In this classroom, there is a dramatic play area, which is set up for housekeeping play today; you see objects and containers of food products found in the homes of the families in the programs. A mother is sitting at one of the tables helping several children make tortillas for a snack. At group time earlier this week, a grandfather came in to tell the children a story from his culture to the whole group. Today's group time finds the children sitting on the floor with a teacher who is speaking a language other than English. She is using two persona dolls to tell a story. These are dolls the children are familiar with—they already know their names, personalities, and family histories as well as something about their cultures. The story is about something that happened between these two dolls. The story is familiar to the children, because something similar happened recently in the play yard between some of them. The teacher asks the children to help the two dolls resolve their problem, and the children contribute lots of ideas.

Creative teachers have always found ways to bring diversity into the classroom; one way is by using parents as resources. The supply catalogs once offered only a few items representing diversity. Now, of course, you can buy "people" crayons in many skin tones—whereas there used to be only one "flesh-colored" crayon in a box, and it was pale. Community helpers are also diversified.

It isn't just "stuff" that makes an environment an antibias one. An antibias environment is also affected by the attitudes and behaviors of the people in it. Organizational matters affect the environment, too. An organization with the goal of an antibias environment has a variety of people in all levels of positions and job roles—the boss isn't necessarily a European American person, and the cleaning person and gardener aren't new immigrants. Antibias also shows up in the way people communicate with each other, as well as in the attitudes of respect and openness that are displayed.

WHAT TEACHERS CAN DO

- Analyze the environment you are in, and see if it welcomes all people who use it.
- Does it reflect people who don't come into the classroom but who are in the community?
- Consider how to make any environment welcoming and reflective of all people.
- Become aware of your own behaviors that show your biases and prejudices.
- Respect all families, and don't make snap judgments about them.
- Keep a positive attitude in the face of differences.
- Give families credit for having funds of knowledge that may be quite different from your own.
- Learn about their funds of knowledge.
- Involve families—ask them to bring in aspects of their culture.
- Pay attention to what goes on between families in the program, and consider helping them to sort out differences, like you help children. But remember, you can't be all things to all people, so if the role of facilitator for adults doesn't come easily, maybe somebody else should do it.

This classroom is in a rural school on the West Coast that has a number of Spanish-speaking families, mostly from Mexico.

SUNNY VALLEY SCHOOL NEWS

SPECIAL EVENTS

Jason Lopez reports on the Cinco de Mayo Celebration.

On May 5th we celebrated Cinco de Mayo. We had three performances, one by Mrs. Gomez's class, one by Ms. Johnson's class and one by Mr. Smith's class. Mrs. Gomez's class did a song called Rancho Grande. Ms. Johnson's class did a dance. Mr. Smith's class did a play. We learned that Cinco de Mayo is all about how the Mexicans won an important battle. At the assembly, Jerrick Palacov, our student council president gave each classroom their own flower.

Jason Lopez

Taking an antibias approach means recognizing the cultures in the class.

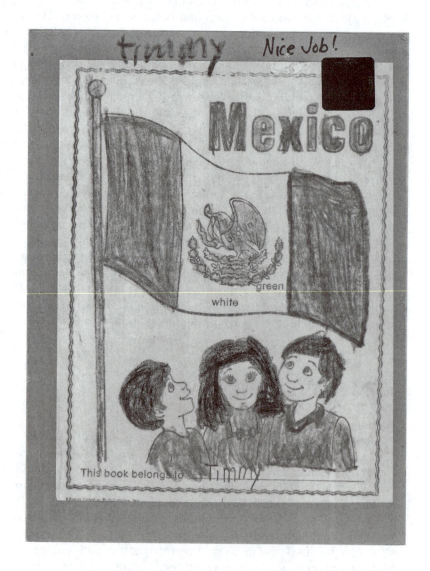

5 RESPECTING ALL FAMILIES, INCLUDING THOSE WITH SAME-SEX PARENTS

WHAT TEACHERS NEED TO KNOW

A book called *Making Room in the Circle: Lesbian, Gay, Bisexual and Transgender Families in Early Childhood Settings* (Lesser et al., 2005) makes it clear that early childhood educators must include all families, even ones they may not know much about. When any families are ignored, the message is strong and invites "silence, invisibility, secrecy, and shame" (Lesser, Burt, and Gelnaw, 2005).

What does it mean to ignore families? It used to be that many families were ignored because classrooms mainly reflected white people of European roots, just as the history books that teachers studied in college told only white history—and only *male* white history at that. That area of ignorance began to be addressed back in the sixties and seventies. But today, LGBT (lesbian, gay, bisexual, and transgender) families are only just beginning to be acknowledged in books and images aimed at early care and education programs and classrooms. According to Lesser, Burt, and Gelnaw (2005), "Children's identities and sense of self are inextricably tied to their families. What happens when children never hear words nor see images that describe their families? . . . [T]he message is clear: 'Your family is just not something to talk about.'"

When children receive unspoken messages that they are not to talk about their families, identity issues can arise. Their school lives and home lives become greatly separated. Self esteem can be affected, which in turn can affect their ability to learn. Even though nobody says their families are unwelcome, the silence gives the message.

It's not enough to just bring in books and images, however. Early childhood educators need to understand the kinds of conditions, including political, legal, and socioeconomic ones, that affect LGBT families. Furthermore, it's important to understand "the dangers that LGBT families face: loss of children, physical violence, danger to their homes and property, unstable employment, financial insecurity and rejections from their families of origin. As educators become aware of these conditions, the ethical responsibility to provide care and safety for children takes on new meaning" (Lesser et al., 2005).

It's also important to know that there are cultural differences in LGBT families and that these may make their lives harder or easier. For example, some Native Americans believe in what are called *two-spirit people*. A two-spirit person has the gift of housing in the body both male and female spirits, which gives that person the ability to see the world from two perspectives.

The goal of your classroom or program should be to create an inclusive learning community where everyone feels safe and has a sense of belonging. Strategy 6 discusses how to do that through building partnerships. Those approaches apply to programs that have LGBT families as well; in addition, consider the approaches listed below.

WHAT TEACHERS CAN DO

- Recognize that a goal for quality education and care programs is for all children to feel good about themselves. One way for teachers to support that feeling is to accept a child's family even though the teacher may not approve of that family. It is imperative that children not receive negative messages about their families!
- Family-centered programs provide the best education and support for children. To be family centered, early childhood professionals partner with all families, including LGBT ones.

- Create an environment of safety and trust. Confidentiality is an important part of such an environment.
- Create a welcoming environment that invites relationship building among *all* families and between families and teachers or staff.
- Unlearn any biases you have around sexual orientation and gender identity. Oppression is oppression, and you don't want to have any part of it—either by supporting oppressive systems, practicing discrimination yourself, or harboring internal oppression.
- Learn the appropriate language related to LGBT families. Don't assume you know what anyone wants to be called; find out. The glossary in Lesser, Burt, and Gelnaw (2005, pp. 9–14) is almost sure to teach you something you don't know.
- Recognize that LGBT parents have struggles most other parents don't, such as asserting their right to exist as a family or keeping their family secret for the safety of their children. They also face a different set of legal issues around marriage, employment benefits, adoption, as well as divorce and child custody.
- Recognize that taking on challenges makes you stronger. Struggling with your own beliefs and honoring *all* families at the same time may seem overwhelming. If the struggle isn't within you, you may find it among colleagues, between them and families, or among the families themselves. It may be hard to facilitate relationships with these struggles going on, but you have to do your best.
- A simple strategy for respecting all families is to check out your forms. Do they have spaces for the mother's name and the father's name, or do they simply indicate parents' names?
- Watch out for events like Mother's Day and Father's Day when not all children have connections with a mother or a father. This issue doesn't just apply to LGBT families. Many children live in single-parent families with no connection to the other parent. How about skipping Mother's Day and Father's Days, and just celebrating Parents' Day?
- Address the family's strengths, not their weaknesses. Like all families, LGBT families have their unique strengths. In addition, they may have some strengths that are directly related to the challenges they face, such as the ability to express who they really are, a willingness to take risks and move toward new forms and social structures, a deep desire and commitment to becoming a parent; as well as resilience and the ability to stand up to discrimination.

6 BUILDING PARTNERSHIPS

WHAT TEACHERS NEED TO KNOW

Partnerships with families are not a given in schools and other early care and education programs. Indeed, if you explore the images of the relationship between early childhood professionals and families, you may find a great variety of them. Expert/amateur, professional/client, and server/served are some images (perhaps unconscious) that lie in the heads of professionals. True partnerships don't fit into any of those images. Partnerships require two-way interactions and commitment. They don't come from the top down.

The partners don't have to be alike; they don't have to have the same skills. In fact, partnerships work better when the partners have different strengths—strengths that complement each other. But one thing both sides need is to have a sense of power in the relationship.

If a partnership is to exist, it is the teacher, caregiver, or director's job to initiate it. So in some ways, unless mandated, the partnership depends on the professional to make it happen. Let's examine what the professional needs to have to create and support partnerships:

1. A strong sense of a particular kind of professionalism. The usual image of a professional is a bit cold and distant. Business clothes may be part of the image. Most early childhood professionals don't fit that image, and if they are to be partners with parents, they can't. They need to create relationships, and that means they can't be cold and distant. They must be warm and personable.

2. Self-respect and respect for others are two key ingredients of a professional/family partnership.

3. Clarity about the importance of building partnerships, and a commitment to do so.

4. Sensitive, self-reflective, and with good coping skills.

Partnerships with families benefit all and serve the child better than when professionals and families work separately to provide early care and education. The family knows their child in a different way than the professional knows the child. Family members have information about the past and present that the professional doesn't. They have visions of a future. They know the child in a greater number of settings than the professional does. The professional knows about children in general—maybe way more than the family does—but not about this particular child in this family. The professional knows how this child behaves in an early childhood environment among peers and with unrelated adults when away from the family. It takes all this information, knowledge, and experience coming together to give the best care and education to each child.

When children see that their teacher or caregiver is working together with their family, they feel more secure. The more the teacher or caregiver and the family work together, the more likely there is to be consistency between what goes on at home and what goes on in the center or at school. The child is likely to feel more comfortable when away from home if the care and education setting is in harmony with the home. The younger the child, the more important the consistency. It's hard for very young children to understand that they should behave differently in one place than they behave in another, though children do grow to have that understanding and, by the primary grades, most children understand about school behaviors (even though they may not always go along with them). The question is, then, is it good for every child to have to adjust to what may feel like an alien setting at first?

When children see that their teacher or caregiver is working together with their parents or guardians, they feel more secure. With a partnership, there is likely to be more consistency between what goes on at home and what goes on in the center.

Professionals gain from putting effort into building partnerships by learning more about family differences and traditions. They gain anthropological information as they experience cultural differences. They can do a better job and achieve more satisfaction when they put themselves in partnership with parents.

Taking a partnership approach benefits parents and other family members by giving them a greater understanding of how early childhood education works in general and in their child's program specifically. By getting involved in the program, family members gain increased knowledge of their own child in a different setting and can visualize what it is like when they aren't there. They can also carry on at home and expand on what the child is involved in at school or at the center. Parents tend to exhibit self-confidence and feel good about their child expanding his or her horizons and skills as he or she pursues new interests and projects.

There are many strategies for forming partnerships with parents. In fact, every one of the strategies in this book is related to reaching that goal of partnerships. Four more are presented below.

WHAT TEACHERS CAN DO

- If you don't already have support systems, work to create some. To create partnerships with parents, you need support from the following:
  - ○ Those above you, like your principal, director, board, or advisory council
  - ○ Policies and a stated philosophy about the value of partnerships with families, and some concrete ways to support it
  - ○ Colleagues you can consult with and talk to
- Find time for communication. Partnerships won't happen if you never have time to talk to parents. This strategy takes more than just a willingness. That's where advocacy comes in. (See Strategies 12 and 13) You need support in the form of such things as extra staff, which is a budget issue that you alone can't solve.
- Hone your communication skills. Partnerships depend on clear communication around mutual expectations. Exchange of information is vital to partnerships.
- Figure out a variety of ways to involve parents. The more flexible you are, the more likely you are to get more parents participating.

7 REMOVING BARRIERS TO PARTNERSHIPS

WHAT TEACHERS NEED TO KNOW

Some of the biggest barriers in communicating and working effectively with families are the attitudes of many early childhood professionals toward families and families' attitudes toward them. Some early childhood education professionals have a bias against parents—setting themselves above the group with whom they are supposed to work. This may be an unconscious attitude, but it comes out in behaviors. It also shows up in language when professionals generalize. Conscious or unconscious stereotypes get in the way of forming partnerships with parents as well. For example, the following has been heard in staff meetings more than once—"Oh, you know how parents are," said with a sigh. That's a generalization. "Oh, those parents," said critically, can indicate a stereotypical idea that parents of a certain group don't really care about their children.

Looking into the reasons behind a negative attitude toward families, we can see a pattern that has come down through the ages. When one group feels downtrodden, lacks self-esteem, and is devalued by society, members of that group sometimes look around to see who they can regard as even lower than themselves. Because of the humble beginnings of early care and education as a field, practitioners have not garnered the esteem (such as it is) of teachers in higher levels of education. Indeed, those who work with children under 5 are even sometimes regarded as babysitters. One U.S. president suggested that child care could be replaced by volunteers, grandmothers, and other kindly community women so that the taxes going into public-supported child care could be saved. One huge argument against such a step is that care and education can never be separated. Another is that training makes a difference in quality. Though early childhood education professionals have nothing to be ashamed of, many of those who work with children under 5 still have difficulty feeling good about themselves, especially when the pay of teachers isn't as high as that of other professionals and the average preschool teacher or child care provider, even those with bachelor's and master's degrees, keeps them at the poverty level on the economic scale.

While professionals are trying to establish their professionalism, they may stress their funds of knowledge and ignore those of the family. They may also take on airs they consider to be professional—such as remaining cool, distant, and emotionally detached. As a profession, early care and education is still exploring what it means to be professional and retain their status while building relationships with each other and with the families and children who are served. Being too emotional and closely attached becomes a problem, but remaining distant, removed, and detached is also a problem.

The other side of the picture is how some family members treat early childhood education professionals. One explanation may be that some family members find themselves much higher on the socioeconomic ladder and look down on their child's teacher or other early care and education staff or provider. They are used to having power at work and may see the people who work with their children as underlings. One infant-toddler care teacher, when told she had to wear an apron, refused to do so, because she in no way wanted to suggest to the parents that she was like their maid.

Another explanation for negative attitudes of parents toward teachers and care and education providers may be that the family perceives they are in the same boat and have the same low status. Family members may seek to rise above that level so they can look down on the early care and education staff or provider.

Whoever designed this space for parents had a good attitude toward them. Often there is no reception area in classrooms or early care and education centers. This one has comfortable seating for the whole family—a real bonus!

WHAT TEACHERS CAN DO

- Become aware of when you are generalizing, and catch yourself. When one parent is making things difficult, it's not uncommon for the early care and education professional to complain to a colleague about parents in general. Remember, just because one parent is giving you difficulties doesn't mean that all parents are the same.
- Avoid stereotyping. Just by living in a racist and sexist society, we unconsciously take in stereotypes. The media is full of them—for example, making fun of people with accents or with differing abilities. Become aware of your own stereotypes, and move beyond them. Making an effort to know individuals from a group that you have a tendency to stereotype will broaden your view of them.
- When someone bothers you, do some self-reflection. Often the traits in people we don't like are the same traits we have in ourselves but don't see. They may not show because we are so busy suppressing them, but when they appear in others, it touches us deeply, where we are most vulnerable. This is called *projection*, and is shows up in the saying that we are more like our worst enemies than our friends.
- Be aware of how powerful roles are. The teacher who is also a parent can forget that when relating to parents in his or her program.
- Work on your own self-esteem. Take care of yourself. Stand up for yourself. Learn self-assertion skills.
- Work on your professionalism. As a member of the early childhood education profession, you are part of something bigger than yourself.
- Recognize that the body of knowledge you have or are gaining is important. Even though you want to be open and sensitive to parents who don't know what you know doesn't mean that you should discount your own knowledge.

Here's a story about how strong the roles we play can be and how they influence our behavior: An early childhood educator who was also a parent went to her daughter's school for a parent-teacher conference. Though she was friends with her daughter's teacher and had talked to him a number of times, once she got into the classroom, she began to feel different. She wasn't there as a friend; she was there as a parent. When she sat on the little chair on the other side of the table, she felt intimidated, even though she was aware that it was partly the furniture influencing her. When the teacher got out his grade book, her daughter's folder, and his notes, she felt stiff and uncomfortable. He seemed to feel the same. Again, she was aware that the roles they were both playing were influencing their interactions. Once the conference was over and the teacher offered her a cookie, the tone of the meeting changed. When she got up to walk out, she was herself again. She was conscious of what was happening while it was happening, but couldn't seem to lighten up the situation.

8 MINIMIZING COMPETITION WITH PARENTS

WHAT TEACHERS NEED TO KNOW

A huge barrier to a working relationship is a feeling of competition between professionals and families. Sometimes parents observe that their child behaves much better around the teacher or early care provider than around them. This can make parents feel insecure. It's important that professionals acknowledge to themselves and to parents that some of the reasons for this difference are less about skills and more about attachment. When children feel insecure and afraid, they may be scared to act out. As soon as the parent arrives, they once again feel secure and less inhibited. This feeling can result in difficult behavior. Also, the child has a closer relationship with the parent, which means that emotions can be passionate or intense. The child who exhibits only mild anger around the teacher or provider can experience a meltdown when the parent is present. It may be that the professional has skills the parents don't, but these other two reasons need to be taken into consideration.

Another factor is that early childhood practitioners who work with children under age 5 have a poor public image and are even called *babysitters* by some. Couple that situation with low wages, and the result may be that the practitioner becomes defensive. As early childhood practitioners seek to establish themselves as true professionals, they may flaunt their knowledge and power. Parents who feel insecure in their parenting competencies may look to the professional as someone who is more competent and more knowledgeable than they are.

A very touchy issue between parents and professionals is competition for the love of the child—whether such is real or only perceived. This competition can be very damaging to a relationship between the adults. It's hard sometimes for teachers, or anybody working with young children, not to compete with parents for children's affection, because that affection is so rewarding. Although attachment to adults in the early care and education program is important, especially in younger children, even parents who are aware of that fact may still feel pangs of jealously if they perceive that competition exists.

Are these two competing for this child's attention? It looks like they might be.

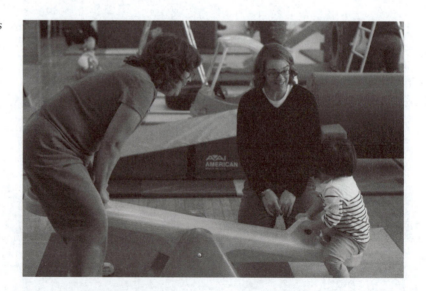

WHAT TEACHERS CAN DO

- Give credit to families for their funds of knowledge. Even though the early childhood professional may be an expert on children in general, families are the experts on their own children. Both kinds of expertise need to come together if the best care and education for young children is to be provided.
- Reassure the families they are number one in the child's life, and that you are well aware of that fact.
- Be aware of when you might be creating competitive situations.
- Watch out for creating excessive emotional dependence in the children. When children care too much about a teacher, it can be hard on the teacher and on the parents.
- Be aware of your own emotional dependence on the children. One teacher who was absent for two days confessed that she was hurt the children didn't miss her more than they did.
- Be sensitive to physical affection between yourself and the children if it seems to bother a particular parent.
- Notice any "child-saving" tendencies in yourself. Become aware of any feelings of rescuing the child from the family. That's not unusual in people who work with young children in early care and education programs. Sometimes it represents a stage that will pass as the person develops professionally. We can't help our feelings, but we can be honest with ourselves about them and stop ourselves from acting on them.

I remember when I was caught in the grasp of what I think of as a "savior complex." I was a new preschool teacher and was out to save many children from their parents (not all—some parents I approved of—the ones like me). Not only was I in the child-saving business, I was going to save the whole world through my work with children by raising a generation that was better than the last one. I was definitely riding on a high horse. I am glad to say I moved out of that stage once I realized parents play a much more important role in children's lives than I ever would, and that I needed to team up with them, not look down on them.

9   SUPPORTING ATTACHMENT

WHAT TEACHERS NEED TO KNOW

Although issues around attachment to teachers and other early care and education practitioners can create difficulties in parent-professional relationships, attachment is important for all children. The younger the child, the more attachment comes into the picture in early care and education programs. In infant-toddler programs, creating a relationship with one or a few special people is vital. Even if infants and toddlers have a firm and close attachment at home, they still need a relationship that is personal, steady, and ongoing if they spend more than a few hours each time away from the family. Feelings of trust and a sense of security come from attachment.

Research being done on the human brain points to the importance of attachment and caring relationships, especially in the first years of life. Bruce Perry (2006), in his lectures and writings, talks about the chemicals that wash over the brain and cause damage when babies experience continual abuse and neglect or live in unusually stressful environments. Without attachment, babies suffer. With a firm, healthy attachment, the baby has a better chance of getting through the hard times with less damage (Perry, 2006). The Pikler Institute, a residential nursery for infants and toddlers in Budapest, Hungary, is based on the concept that attachment to caregivers is a vital ingredient of the first years of life, and that it allows even institutionalized babies to grow up to be whole, healthy, and fully functioning adults. David and Appell (2001) Gonzalez-Mena (2004), Petrie and Owen (2005), as well as Shonkoff and Phillips (2000) have made a strong case for caring relationships. When babies feel secure in a healthy attachment, their brains are able to develop without harmful chemicals interfering with the process. Studies of resilient children indicate that even just one close and caring relationship can make a difference even in the face of continual hardship (Werner, 1995).

Attachment to a caregiver, a teacher, or a provider is a concern for many families. "Will my children still love me if they spend all that time away from me while I'm working" is an agonizing question many parents ask themselves. Teachers and caregivers should be reassuring if they perceive that a parent has this concern.

When families watch their children get attached to someone outside the family, they may have conflicting feelings. For some, it is a relief that their child feels comfortable and safe away from home, but mixed with that can come feelings of being replaced. Some families feel competition for the child's affection. When caregivers and teachers seem to know more, have better skills, and can handle their children better than the families can, the feelings of competition can be devastating.

Lilian Katz (1977) reminds us that being a teacher, caregiver, or provider is very different from being a parent, though children should be attached to both. The following are some of the differences:

- The child's attachment to the family is and should be closer than the attachment to the professionals.
- The child has both a history and a future with the family. The relationship of the early childhood professional is more short term, with the exception of some family child care providers who may work with the same child for 11 or 12 years, and with the family for even longer if there are siblings. But even then, the future of the child is still in the hands of the family, not in those of the professional.
- The length of the relationship of child to the early childhood professional is less predictable. Children can leave the program at any time if the family changes programs or moves away from the school.

Attachment is important for all children. The younger the child, the more attachment comes into the picture in early care and education programs.

As children grow older, if they have a firm sense of themselves and feel secure in their attachments at home, most don't need such a close, one-on-one relationship with an adult in out-of-home programs. Kindergarten and primary teachers have a larger group size and ratio of children to adults, so the amount of one-on-one personal attention drops compared to that in prekindergarten and infant-toddler programs. Skilled teachers who understand the value of these relationships can still form healthy attachments even in these situations so that all children feel valued and close to their teacher.

WHAT TEACHERS CAN DO

- Take attachment seriously. If policies to promote attachment aren't already in place, do what you can to create them. Such policies should include:
  - Small group size—The younger the children, the smaller the group needs to be. Starting with infants, a good group size is six infants with two caregivers. This way the caregivers can get to know a reasonable number of children as well as their families (Lally, 1995). As children get older, the group size can increase. In some states, 20 is considered a reasonable group size for K-3.
  - Primary caregivers—Especially for children under age 3, each professional should have several children for whom he or she is primarily responsible and works to become attached to. This is not an exclusive relationship, and there should be other caregivers who also know the children individually and as a group (Lally, 1995). By kindergarten, especially if children have learned to be functioning members of a peer group, one teacher will work, though it is desirable to have several adults, including some parent volunteers, in the classroom. That way children get more individualized attention from adults. Family participation is another benefit.

- ○ Continuity of care—This is a concept that applies more to infants and toddlers and, to some extent, preschoolers than the those in K-3, though some schools use what's called a *looping system*. Continuity of care, or *looping*, means keeping children together for longer periods rather than promoting them to a new room and teacher. In some programs, infants and toddlers are moved (or promoted) on a regular basis each time they reach a new stage of development or have a birthday instead of staying together as a group with the same teacher. Keeping the group together with the teacher means that as infants and toddlers outgrow the environment, the environment either needs to change or the group and teachers need to move together to a new room. For infants and toddlers, two or three years gives them and their parents a chance to become attached to the professionals.

- Communicate with the family about the policies and their purpose. Explain clearly that the attachment to the early childhood professional is not meant to compete with the attachment to the family. The family attachment should always be closer because it is far more important and long-lasting than any other attachment.

- Support the child's attachment to family, and acknowledge the child's feelings for the family members to whom he or she is most attached. Assure parents that they are number one in the child's life.

- Be aware that some families may feel threatened by seeing evidence that their children care about their teachers, and do what you can to help these families feel more secure. Watch out for the following pitfalls:

  - ○ Encouraging lots of physical affection from children, especially if you see the parent looking uncomfortable when the child comes back for yet another hug and kiss.

  - ○ Letting a child call you mommy or daddy. Correct them if they do. Let parents help you decide by what name you should be called.

  - ○ Taking pride in being the first to see a child reach a milestone. "Your baby took his first step today" can be a devastating announcement to parents who wished they could be there to see it. Let the parent make the discovery that the baby is starting to walk and announce it to you.

- Look inside yourself, and explore your own feelings about a particular child or family. It's natural for professionals to have strong feelings about a child or group of children. Some professionals go through a "savior stage" of wanting to rescue children from their parents. Acknowledge your feelings, and at the same time, become fully aware of your actions. You can *accept* the feelings without *acting on* them.

- Understand that professionals establishing attachment should focus on optimal distance while promoting optimal closeness in family attachment.

10 CONSIDERING AUTHORITY

WHAT TEACHERS NEED TO KNOW

One issue that sometimes comes up between early childhood education professionals and families is the question of who is the authority in what situation. In school, when a parent is there and the child breaks a rule, should the parent step back and let the teacher handle it, or should the parent take care of it? In a family child care home, when a child starts jumping on the couch, is it the parent's place to stop the child (even if jumping on the couch is allowed at their home), or is it the provider's job? At an open house at school when children come with their parents, if the children are out of order, whose job is it to correct them? Or, at a child care center when the staff and parents put on a party for new-comers to get acquainted, the children are invited, and a group of them gets too wild, whose job is it to settle them down?

Sometimes this is not a problem. One party or the other may stepforward and manage the behavior, and both may be in agreement about what is the right thing to do. At other times, both parties wait for the other to do something, resulting in out-of-bounds behavior of the child, lack of guidance, broken rules, and maybe even damaged property. Such situations can also result in a sense of confusion or insecurity on the part of children, who know they are out of bounds and expect someone to do something about it. Alternatively, if one adult steps back and the other steps in because the other isn't doing anything, that action may result in hurt feelings or resentment on the part of one or both adults.

WHAT TEACHERS CAN DO

- Determine who will be the authority in each case. Who has the primary responsibility for the child's behavior in each setting or situation when both parent and professional are present at the same time? This is not something you can look up in a book—it has to be decided among the parties involved.
- Plan ahead, as in the previous story.
- When a situation occurs where the authority issues haven't been settled, discuss the situation out in the open.
- Anticipate situations, and discuss them ahead of time. For example, at a parent meeting, one pre-school center discussed the expectations they had for parents to be in charge of their own children at an upcoming party with family members and staff. The families agreed that it would be up to them, even though the party was taking place in the center, where the teachers usually provided guidance for the children.

Another issue around authority relates to who has what information. The photo on page 89 shows an example of a first-grade teacher discussing a child's progress with his father. In this case, the teacher knows what goes on at school and how the child performs. She not only has her observations and interactions to give her information but also has actual records and samples of the child's work. Just because she has information about the child at school doesn't mean that she ignores what the father knows about the child outside of school. His information is important to her, just as her information is important to him. Notice that the child is part of the conference. This discussion isn't going on behind child's back. It includes his viewpoint, information, and experience as well.

Parents may not have all the information about child development, curriculum, and how to teach groups of children that teachers have, but they do have plenty of information about their own child that the teacher doesn't—the child's history, interests, and their plans for their child's future. They are the authority on how their family works and on being members of their culture. Each has other areas of expertise as well that vary by family and by individual. The following are some strategies for thinking about, respecting, and responding to the authority that lies in the family:

- Respect each family's authority over its own children.
- Get to know family members, and you will discover their many areas of expertise. Some of these people can be resources for your classroom or center.
- Appreciate the funds of knowledge that families have and focus on their strengths. (See Strategy 11, Focusing on Family Strengths.)
- Find ways to share what the families know and what you know. Everybody will be richer.

11   FOCUSING ON FAMILY STRENGTHS

WHAT TEACHERS NEED TO KNOW

When a family you are trying to build a partnership with is struggling with many challenges, you try to empathize with them. You seek to understand what it is like to walk in their shoes. Perhaps, at the same time, you think about the ways you can help them and also consider the resources the community has to offer. All these approaches are valid, but they also lead you to focus on the family's problems instead of its strengths. Turnbull and Turnbull (2001) said, "Highlighting and appreciating families' strengths is one of the key aspects of supporting families to enhance their own self-efficacy" (p. 67).

A key to working with all families is to be sensitive, understanding, empathetic, and remember their strengths. You're not a therapist, but you can be an ally. Just by listening and talking, you can show your support. By having faith that people can use their own abilities to succeed in life in spite of obstacles, you can help them heal. Think about people in your own life who have believed in your strengths and recognized your potential.

It may be hard to shift focus from problems to strengths, but think about the approaches described below that you can take to make such a shift.

"Highlighting and appreciating families' strengths is one of the key aspects of supporting families to enhance their own self-efficacy" (Turnbull & Turnbull, 2001, p. 67).

WHAT TEACHERS CAN DO

- Look at how you are defining the family. Can you see how they are unique and special instead of downtrodden and miserable? Are you aware of the skills, strengths, and special talents that each member has? Think about their resources.

- If you don't know enough about the family to see its strengths, do you have ways to find out? Having conversations with family members is one way. You may not have much time to talk to families, but if you are dedicated to partnerships with parents, you know that conversations are essential if you are to get to know and appreciate each family.

- Storytelling is another way to learn about family strengths. When we hear each other's stories, it makes us remember our own. Stories can be healing. As you listen to stories, remember to think in terms of possibilities instead of dwelling on problems.

- The challenges that individuals and families face do not necessarily weaken them. Sometimes these challenges give them the strength and courage to grow, develop, and move forward. Don't assume that challenges always result in damage.

- Help the family keep their focus on their dreams and aspirations instead of on what is happening right now. Help them concentrate on a life without the challenges they face at the moment. If they can visualize that life, they can aim for it.

- You may have expertise, but the real experts in this family are the members themselves. Help them tune in to the expertise they have.

- Help the family members empower themselves by making them aware of the choices they have. (See Strategy 29, Empowerment.)

Perhaps the child who drew this picture comes from a family that has a love of music as one of its strengths.

- You may have resources to offer, but help the family members tune in on their own resources and focus on their strengths, skills, and potentials.
- Focus on protective factors rather than on risk factors. For example, a family who has a broad base of support for the parents and is a member of a community has an important protective factor to stand up against the risk factor of ill health or a financial crisis.

What are some strengths that families show even when they have big problems? Here are some samples of strengths families can have—either as a group or as individuals within the family:

1. Strong attachment that shows up as love for their children and is reciprocated.
2. An extended family network that they can rely on.
3. The ability to speak two languages plus one dialect.
4. Good social skills.
5. Persistence and stubbornness. They don't give up.
6. Physical strength, body awareness, good health habits.
7. A strong sense of humor.
8. A love of making music and listening to it.
9. A cheerful outlook.
10. A variety of interests.
11. "Street smarts." They know how to get along and keep safe.
12. Mutual support.
13. A knowledge of how to "work the system."

12 HELPING PARENTS TO BE ADVOCATES FOR THEIR CHILDREN

WHAT TEACHERS NEED TO KNOW

A role for family members that comes naturally to some, but not all, is to advocate for their own child. For those family members who don't see themselves in this role, it's up to the teacher or other early childhood professional to help them understand that they have a right to be their child's advocate.

How does a family show that they are advocating for their child? When a parent comes to the teacher with concerns about her child, she is being an advocate. If a parent sees the teacher at the end of the day and asks how the day went, he is usually asking about his own child, not as much about the teacher's day. It's not that he doesn't care about the teacher or want to know about the rest of the class; he mostly wants information that relates to his own child. When parents focus on their own children, they are being advocates for their children.

When family members stand up for their own child in the face of all the others, their attitude may put them in opposition to the professionals whose role is to advocate for the group rather than singling out one child in that group. For example, a family who doesn't celebrate any holidays asks for a meeting with the second-grade teacher whose curriculum is built around holidays and seasons. The teacher may think, "Why doesn't it seem unreasonable to this family member that the other children be denied their pleasure for the sake of a single child?" When the teacher understands that families are advocates for their own children, then the request or demand makes sense. Another example in a preschool occurred when one family member who comes from a culture where women stay covered up complained about her four-year-old daughter running around without a shirt on, which was common practice in the program on warm days. Still another family member who came from a state where there are hookworms in the soil complained about his child running around barefoot and wanted the child's shoes left on at all times. Neither request is unreasonable. Yet both requests make it hard on the teacher—first, to remember the individual requests, and then, to carry them out when most of the other children are shirtless and shoeless. It becomes even harder when the two children concerned want to join the crowd and do what the rest of the children are doing.

Although it may seem wrong to make exceptions or to change a whole program for one child, think about the idea of including children with special needs in a classroom set up for typically developing children. Individualizing can be as important for *all* children and families as it is for those with special needs. Parents are the ones who can help the teacher individualize by advocating for their children.

It's important, when thinking about families as advocates for their children, to be fully aware that being a parent is very different from being a teacher. Keeping this fact in mind is vital to working well with families. One difference, according to Lilian Katz, is that families are particularistic—they favor their own children over others, have an emotional stake in their children's welfare, are biased in favor of their own children, and put their the needs of their own children first, even at the expense of other children's needs. Early childhood education professionals must be universalistic—be concerned about every child in the class or group without bias, not put any one child first at the expense of the others, and apply skills and resources to each child.

WHAT TEACHERS CAN DO

- Appreciate when parents stand up for their own child. This is a healthy kind of bias, even though it may make your job more difficult. All children need an advocate who takes their side.
- Support families in their role as an advocate for their child.
- Help families who don't have strong advocacy tendencies to acquire them. Part of this approach involves asking them about their child on an ongoing basis.
- At the very beginning of your relationship with the family, ask what their goals are for their child. Better yet, ask what their *dreams* are for their child. Erma Bombeck, a humorous author, wrote, "It takes a lot of courage to show your dreams to someone else." That's why forming a relationship and building trust with families is so important! Asking parents about their dreams for their children is an approach that Jean Monroe, national early childhood consultant and trainer based in California, suggests. Parents who discuss their dreams rather than their goals for their child tend to set their sights higher. After you ask, really listen to what they have to say. Make it a point to always listen to them when they talk about their child.
- See the families' natural tendency toward advocacy as something that can be expanded to advocacy for the program in the face of budget cuts, for example. (See Strategy 13, Encouraging Parents to Becoming Advocates for All Children.)
- When the family's advocacy tendencies conflict with your perspective, practice holding their perspective in mind as well as your own. It's a matter of becoming self-aware—observing yourself from a distance even when engaged in an emotional conversation. Keep reminding yourself that it's good they are advocating for their child.
- Be flexible. Acknowledge that there are whole realms of possibilities in addition to the ways you are comfortable with or have always done things.
- Learn win-win negotiation skills (See Strategy 15, Understanding and Appreciating Cultural Differences)
- Keep in mind the differences in roles between parent and professional. Your relationship with the child is short term and can end abruptly. You don't have a history or a long-term future. You're not the parent.

Parents who participate in early care and education programs tend to be advocates for their own children, and some go on to become advocates for children in general.

13 ENCOURAGING PARENTS TO BECOME ADVOCATES FOR ALL CHILDREN

WHAT TEACHERS NEED TO KNOW

When looking at partnerships, families who advocate for the program stand out! Some of these families started out by advocating for their own children (see Strategy 12, Helping Parents to Be Advocates for Their Children) and then ended up becoming advocates for the group of children of which their child is a member. A natural progression for some families is to focus on their own child and then later on the class or group their child is in. Some move beyond that to advocating for the entire school or program. Other families skip all those steps and become advocates for children in general.

The importance of child advocacy is a lesson that many who enter the field of early care and education learn, whether they are professionals or parents. Children can't speak for themselves, so adults have to speak for them. When budget cuts come to school districts or child care programs, who can speak for the children? When school districts or state departments of education mandate curriculum that is developmentally inappropriate, culturally inappropriate, or harmful in other ways, who can speak for children? The voices most heard are those of parents—the consumers. Some families are natural advocates and understand the process. They will protest on their own, without urging, when their children can't get what they need from the powers that be. Other families have to learn to be advocates. They can learn a good deal from those who teach in or run the schools or other early childhood education programs their children attend.

Advocacy can start close to home and feel uncomfortable for the professionals at first when they are a target, such as when the families are advocating for the teacher or program to change. One example was reported by Jim Greenman (reported in Gonzalez-Mena, 2008a). A group of African American parents got together and told their teachers that they didn't want their children to go outside anymore. The teachers started a parent education campaign to make sure the parents understood the influence of gross motor development on cognition and the importance of fresh air and exercise to health. They continued with the outdoor program, but the parents continued demanding a change. It wasn't until the two sides finally sat down together and the teachers asked the parents what was behind their demand that the true problem came out into the open. It was the sandbox. Children were coming home with sand in their hair, which was causing all kinds of problems, including rashes, ringworm on the scalp, even damage to the hair. When the two groups put their heads together and started brainstorming solutions, they came up with one—shower caps for children who play in the sandbox. (See Strategy 21 for more about conflict resolution.)

Though this particular situation put families and professionals on opposite sides at first, they eventually ended up on the same side, with everybody focusing on what was best for the children. Even when the ending isn't so satisfying, the fact that parents mobilize themselves must be seen in a positive light. When parents find energy as a group to push for change, that energy can be used again when an issue comes up that the program faces. If the funds are cut and the program is in jeopardy, it's possible that the families will team up with the teachers and advocate to save it.

What can families advocate for? Marion Wright Edelman (2003), who founded the Children's Defense Fund, evaluated the progress made since 1973 in key areas related to the lives of children and created a report card that pointed out there is still much to be done. Poverty got the worst grade of the key areas, rating a grade of D, because although in 1973 one out of six children lived in poverty, the rate had risen to one in five by 2003. In a 2000 UNICEF report, the United States ranked next to last among industrialized nations in child poverty. Its infant mortality rate (another key area) put the United States 28th among industrialized nations (far behind France and Germany). Gun violence

Some parents and other family members start out by advocating for their own children and then connect with other families to advocate for the group of children of which their child is a member.

was another key area. Although child gun deaths have dropped since 1973, an American child today is 12 times more likely to die from gunfire than a child in any other industrialized country. There is much work for child advocates to do to improve the lives of children and their families.

What are some approaches to helping parents along the road to advocacy for all children?

WHAT TEACHERS CAN DO

- Realize that families organizing and advocating can be beneficial even though you may disagree with the target of their advocacy efforts. Keep in mind how effectively that energy can be used when you are all on the same side.
- Help families see the big picture. Advocating for children involves speaking out for giving all children access to high-quality, developmentally and culturally appropriate early childhood educational experiences in rich, safe environments. There is great inequality in schools, and that needs to change. Programs for children under 5 may not have well-trained or well-paid teachers. That needs to change as well. Child advocates have made progress and will continue to do so, especially if their numbers continue to grow with the addition of families who are served by schools and other early care and education programs.
- Encourage advocacy even when the need isn't evident, and teach parents how to be effective advocates. Recognize all the places that advocacy works, such as school boards and other governing bodies, regulatory agencies, and lawmakers at the community, state, and even the national level. Early childhood education has benefited greatly in the past from family advocacy efforts.
- If families don't organize themselves, help them. Recognize potential leaders among families, and nurture their leadership qualities. Start by brushing up on your own leadership skills. Debra Sullivan's 2003 book *Learning to Lead* has many useful ideas.
- Help families understand the many courses of advocacy action. The following are just a few suggestions:
  - ○ Creating or joining an advocacy group
  - ○ Collecting information about a critical issue
  - ○ Finding and sharing research that relates to the issue, and formulating a position statement
  - ○ Forming or joining a legislative telephone or e-mail tree
  - ○ Keeping up with the issue in the media, and writing letters to the editor
  - ○ Understanding how laws are made
  - ○ Developing a relationship with lawmakers, and keeping in touch with them about the issues that concern children and families

One Person Can Make a Difference

Here is a story about what one town did to respond to child abuse in their community (Gonzalez-Mena, 2009): When a baby died as the result of abuse, a group of residents, led by one individual, decided to do something. This was in the time when child abuse was just beginning to be recognized as widespread and a threat to children's mental and physical health. Though laws were in place at this time, the laws were not enough for this particular group of citizens, who wanted to prevent abuse in their community, not just punish it. This motivation on their part coincided with some funding set aside for prevention, intervention, and treatment of child abuse. The group went to work.

First, they established a hotline for parents to call, just to talk, when they felt as though they might not be able to control themselves. Then, they began to educate the community about child abuse and about using the hotline. This group soon discovered that what parents needed was a variety of support services. Some needed parenting information and skills, some needed relief child care, some needed a job, some needed a place to live, and some just needed relief from the many stresses in their lives that led them to take out their frustrations on their children. The picture was much bigger than anyone had ever suspected.

Today, many of these services are in place, including parent support and education groups, relief child care, an emergency aid fund, part-time temporary home service with a helper coming into the home to assist with household and child management, and other services. In addition, there is an innovative service called "phone friend" for children who come home from school to an empty house. All this because one person cared and figured out how to involve others in advocacy.

14 CREATING A SENSE OF COMMUNITY

WHAT TEACHERS NEED TO KNOW

Partnering with families is an important goal for teachers and other professionals in early care and education programs. A related goal is to consider building a community out of the partners.

Think of a community as a group of people connected by some common interest or purpose. Going by that definition, a classroom or an early care and education program can certainly become a community. Sometimes it happens naturally, but usually it takes a little effort to facilitate the making of those connections. It doesn't have to be hard. Think of how a good hostess moves among guests, introducing them to each other and making a group of individuals or couples into a party. Some of the skills that a good hostess has apply directly to the goal of forming children, families, and staff into a community. The purpose is different of course, because the main objective is not just a social one but, rather, an enhancement of the children's educational experience. Also, the focus is longer than a party—not just for an evening but for perhaps a year or even more. Sometimes the connections families make with each other in early care and education programs last for a lifetime!

In 1980, Ethel Seiderman cofounded an organization called the Parent Services Project as a way to support families. The idea was to focus on families instead of just on children. In a book about the Parent Services Project called *Stronger Together*, Lisa Lee (2004) explains the benefits of community building. "One of the gifts of family-centered programs is the creation of caring communities. Connected to one another by their children, adults in such places care about and help one another . . . Families use the center as a place to connect with one another. When good things happen for one family, everyone celebrates. When problems occur, people are concerned and work together . . . [I]n such a place, children grow up feeling safe, covered in a quilt of warmth from the adults in their lives."

So how do early childhood professionals turn a group of people into a community? Seiderman is a master at turning groups into communities, and she has been doing it for a number of years, starting before the Parent Services Project when she was a child care director and ran a family-centered child care program. Her idea was to support the parents in supporting the child. That idea is blossoming in schools and other early childhood education programs across the United States, partly because of Seiderman's long-time commitment to changing the focus from the child to the family and from the family by itself to the community as a whole. Seiderman says that the Parent Services Project emphasizes the idea that parenting is not just a private concern of the family but a communitywide concern. One way to broaden the parenting role is to give teachers and parents new ways of supporting each other.

Marion Cowee, a preschool director for many years, explains how to create a community from a group of families (Cowee, 2005). "You have to make sure that everybody has a sense of belonging." Cowee doesn't mean just the parents—she suggests "finding out who are the potential members of this community. Include everyone who is important in each child's life, including grandparents, aunts, and nannies." She makes clear that the goal is to help everyone feel they belong in your classroom or program. Marion and long-time toddler and preschool teacher Lynne Doherty, who has taught in early childhood programs for many years, contributed to the following list of strategies.

Your attitude makes a difference. If you are trying to build a sense of belonging, you will invite family members in regularly. One way is by having an open-door policy that encourages family members to drop in whenever they want. Some teachers have a strong reaction to that idea, however, and consider it too disruptive. Kitty Ritz, a first-grade teacher, has solved that problem. Twice a week, she sets aside a half hour at the beginning of the day for family reading time in her classroom. This is one of the many ways that she gets to know the parents and they get to know each other. That's another secret to minimizing disruptions when family members come to visit—get them involved in productive ways that don't disturb the children. Make them part of the children's routine.

The following are additional ways to create a sense of belonging and make the kinds of connections that turn a group into a community.

WHAT TEACHERS CAN DO

- Create a sense of belonging from the beginning by finding out what everybody with whom you come in contact wants to be called. Then, work on learning all the names—including the correct pronunciation. This is not an easy job if the program or class is large, but it is a good way for early childhood professionals to work on their own learning skills as models for the children.
- Introduce everyone who is part of the program or a support to the classroom, such as aides, cooks, custodians, or bus drivers.
- Help people get acquainted by putting up a picture board of the staff, with a little something written about each person. It could be a short biography, or a statement of what the person likes about working with children and families, or a list of hobbies. Put this somewhere that families who drop their children off can easily see it. Some programs include substitutes on the picture board as well as regular employees.
- Consider a picture board of families as well, with a few facts or statements about each one. Put this up where staff and other families can see it.
- If the entry area has the space, consider not just a bulletin board for parents, planned and maintained by the staff, but also a bulletin board for parents that they plan, maintain, and interact with. An interactive idea to put on the family bulletin board is a changing survey, with space for family members to write under a question. For example, a question could be "What is your child's favorite restaurant?" This kind of question gives parents something to talk to each other about.
- In a preschool setting, if children arrive with a family member each day, have the room set up for a free play period, and make yourself available to greet children and adults. When children enter an interesting environment, they can separate more easily and also become engaged with the materials and with each other. That gives adults a chance to talk to each other briefly, both at the beginning of the session and at the end. (See Strategy 31, Holding Ongoing Conversations with Families.)
- Introduce families to each other. Note where personal connections are forming, and later on, suggest that maybe the family consider changing the emergency form to include new friends, rather

For family reading time in a first-grade classroom, parents are invited to participate two days a week for the first half hour of the morning.

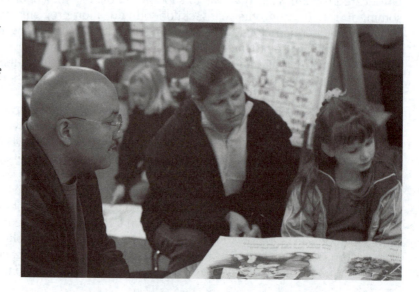

than the distant aunt in another town whom the child barely knows, to come get the child when necessary.

- Help parents become resources for each other. Carpooling is one way they can work together and gain a sense of belonging to a community.

- Use the intake interview, if there is one, to begin getting acquainted, including finding out what special interests or skills family members might have.

- Make sure your environment is welcoming to everybody. (See Strategy 4, Creating an Antibias Environment, for ideas.) A welcoming environment means that images on the walls include every-body, the languages of the families are represented, and adaptations are made for people with disabilities—both children and adults. One program wanted to make sure that all the books they had available for the children gave welcoming messages, so they taped a clean sheet of paper to the inside cover of each book with the suggestion for parents to write their comments and reactions to the book. It soon became clear that what one parent loved, another felt offended by. In this way, both parents and staff learned about differing perspectives about what feels welcoming.

- Having an address list is always a good idea so that families can connect with each other on their own. Be sure you have permission from each family to put their name and contact information on the list.

- Fund-raising is a way for family members to get to know each other by working together. Be careful to recognize that some families have children in more than one class or program. Fund-raising can get to be a burden in a large family.

- Always think of meetings as a way for people to get to know each other, no matter what the purpose of the meeting is. Start with an icebreaker to loosen people up and get them relaxed and interacting. (See Strategy 34 for hints on how to run meetings so that families form relationships with each other.)

- This entire book is full of ideas about how to make families and staff into a community. In particular, look at Strategy 28 for ideas about how to set up the environment for communication, Strategy 22 for ideas about how to get families to participate in the program, and Strategy 6 for ideas about how to build partnerships with families.

A picture board of the families in the program helps to create a welcoming spirit and a feeling of belonging.

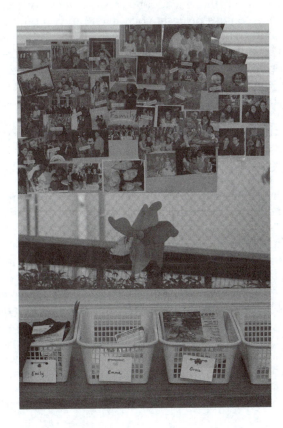

15 UNDERSTANDING AND APPRECIATING CULTURAL DIFFERENCES

WHAT TEACHERS NEED TO KNOW

What is *culture* anyway? "Culture is a shared system of meaning, which includes values, beliefs, and assumptions expressed in daily interactions of individuals within a group through a definite pattern of language, behavior, customs, attitudes, and practices" (Maschinot, 2008, p. 2). A worthy goal is for teachers and other early care and education specialists to become culturally sensitive and begin looking for the meaning of parenting behaviors and beliefs they run across in the families they serve. Though it may seem as if a step toward that goal is to examine lists of cultural traits of various groups, that approach doesn't work. Those lists are generalizations, and generalizations can promote stereotypes.

Understanding cultural differences has to do with recognizing yourself as a cultural being and coming to understand that the way you see the world, organize your behavior, and look at children are, to a great extent, influenced by your own culture, which also may have been influenced by your training. It's hard for teachers and other early care and education professionals (including family child care providers) to know what to do when parenting practices raise questions yet the professional is trying to be culturally sensitive and responsive and to build a good relationship with the parent. How does this professional honor and respect diversity when parenting practices don't fit personal and professional definitions of best practices? How can teachers and providers respect and honor practices that seem to be incomprehensible, bad, wrong, or maybe even harmful?

If you haven't thought about diversity in terms of contradictions, this idea of honoring what seems wrong may confuse or upset you—even put you off balance. Those feelings are not bad—they can serve you well, because when we enter a state of disequilibrium, that's the perfect condition in which to learn something new. If we suspend judgment, we can come to understand that what looks wrong from our personal perspective may look right to someone else. We can learn something by looking through someone else's eyes. It's uncomfortable to begin questioning what we already know, but it's important to do so when working in an early childhood setting that includes diverse families you don't see eye to eye with.

Of course, causing harm to children is not something we can tolerate, but when we really begin to understand another's perspective, we may see how something that seems to hurt children doesn't when regarded in a different context. Instead of just taking the behaviors at face value, our job is to look beneath them to see if we can discover patterns of meaning.

A saying that clarifies this point comes from Dianna Ballesteros, a child care director who is a long-time advocate for the antibias movement in California. Dianna says, "En cada cabeza hay un mundo."—"In each head there is a world." Expanding the world in one's own head is the means to understanding people who are different from one's self, and it goes way beyond just celebrating differences in ethnic foods, music, and customs. By acknowledging that each person has a different reality, you take the first step toward beginning to understand it.

What about the diversity involving child-rearing practices that a teacher considers wrong? Take a family who sends a baby bottle in the lunch box of a kindergartener for snack time. As the teacher gets to know the mother, she realizes that the family is "babying" this child in more ways than one. In the teacher's language, "babying" has negative connotations. The mother and older siblings do everything for the child, which means she is often passive and seldom tries to do anything for herself, including putting on her own coat. When the kindergarten teacher talks to the preschool teacher, who has the same family in her program, the kindergarten teacher discovers that the mother is still spoon-feeding the four-year-old at home, even though both children feed themselves fine when no one is there to help them. The teachers worry to each other about these children's sense of independence—their self-esteem and their competence to take care of themselves. They agree that developing self-help skills is a major task of the early years. "Babying children" like this family is doing harms the children's sense of themselves as individuals!

These teachers are engaged in dualistic thinking, which makes it seem that if their ideas are right and the family has to be wrong. They want to be culturally responsive to the family, but they can't condone what the mother is doing. The teachers are coming from the context of Western culture and perspective, and they have the support of others who have the same kind of background, education, training, and experience. From their view, this family's practice is known to cause harm. They even know the term for the type of harm—it's called *overdependence*, or even *codependence*, and is what results in the need for counseling when children grow up.

From another perspective, neither of these practices is harmful—indeed, these practices are just the opposite. They are not only beneficial but also necessary in view of a particular set of goals. In his 1981 book *Beyond Culture*, Edward Hall, an anthropologist, uses an old saying about "apron strings" to explain differences. He writes, "The world can be divided into those cultures that prepare their children to be independent individuals and live apart from their family of origin as adults and those that do not. Those cultures that do not emphasize independence and individuality prepare their children to remain closely tied to the family as adults, living in close proximity if not in the same house, dwelling, or compound." In other words, one group cuts the apron strings, and the other does not.

For many people trained in early care and education, it is easy to see why cultures cut the apron strings and how they raise their children in preparation for this cutting. For those people, it may be hard see the other view, and they may be extremely resistant to it.

Families who don't cut the apron strings see independence and individuality as a threat, not a goal. They are confident that their children will grow up to be independent, but they worry that they will be *too* independent and leave the family behind in their quest for individuality. So starting at birth, the caregivers in these families dampen the flames of independence when they arise and, instead, teach the value of being dependent and of having others dependent on you.

One way to look at these differences is to regard them as two different patterns of meanings. Names given to these particular patterns vary, but calling the teacher's perspective *individualistic* and the families' perspective *interdependent* is one way to label them (Maschinot, 2008). The families who cut apron strings teach children self-help skills and encourage them to acknowledge the feat. "I did it all by myself" is not considered bragging but as an example of being proud of one's individual accomplishments. Children are encouraged to make individual choices and think for themselves. They are taught to be assertive. The families who are aiming at keeping bonds strong and families together downplay skills showing independence, which they figure are naturally built in and will arise no matter what. Instead of helping children take pride in individual accomplishments, they teach a skill that some would call "graciously accepting help." Children in interdependent families are taught that close connections and collaboration are more important than personal self-development. Lessons in being self-controlled, conforming, and cooperative are important in interdependent families. Respect for elders and putting your needs and desires aside for those of others are also important lessons that children learn in these families—quite a contrast to the individualistic cultures.

People are usually so immersed in their culture that they don't think of why they are doing, what they are doing, only that it feels right. If asked, the parent stressing interdependence might say that they *like* doing things for their children, or maybe that their children are too young to do things for themselves. They might not be able to explain that they are trying to keep their children close to them and create strong, lifelong ties. Most people have a hard time explaining their culture or how their actions and attitudes relate to it.

WHAT TEACHERS CAN DO

- When something about a family's practices really bothers you, try to look at what they are doing through their eyes instead of your own.
- Try to withhold judgment long enough to gain a deeper understanding than first impressions allow.

- Don't just withhold judgment from people who are obviously from a different culture than your own. It may be easier for you to accept differences if you think that people have a valid cultural reason. Consider people of your own culture who think differently from the way you do. Their reality is just as valid as the reality of someone who has a entirely different culture as a backup. Just because the family that is doing what we disagree with is of the same culture as you are doesn't mean that they don't have their own reasons behind their practice. Work as hard to understand them as you would to understand families of cultures different from your own.
- Don't assume that doing things for children will make them grow up helpless and forever dependent. The modeling process is very strong. Children imitate what they see others doing. If one grows up seeing people helping others, they too become helpers, in addition to receivers, of help. Putting that modeling effect together with a lifetime of lessons in respect for elders, you can see that it might result in the youngers helping the elders when the time comes that the elders need help.

Teresa, who was from Mexico and a staff member in a program where I once worked, helped me see a perspective on meeting needs that was different from my own on the subject. I was telling her how important I thought it was for children to learn to meet their own needs as soon as possible. My argument usually went like this: If we meet our own needs, we are more able to help those who can't meet their needs. The flight attendants say in the plane, "In case of a loss of cabin pressure, put on your own oxygen mask before helping others." Behind that statement is the idea that if you lose consciousness, you won't be of any use to anybody else. Well, that's the way I was looking at the issue of meeting needs—we have to look out for ourselves first. And I've never forgotten what Teresa said in response. "Janet, that's so sad. If you are looking out for yourself, that's only one person concerned about you. But if instead of focusing on yourself you think first of others, and if everybody else does the same, that's lots and lots of people looking out for you." That conversation stuck with me. It gave me a new way to think about things. I was able to see her point and honor our differences, but I didn't shift my whole frame of reference to become a person who no longer values independence and individuality. I am still who I am. I still have a particular set of values that relate to the way I was raised, my family of origin, and my culture, which I label as European American, white, Anglo, or Celtic American, depending on to whom I am talking. I am who I am, but I now have a broader perspective on differences.

16 ESTABLISHING CULTURALLY RESPONSIVE EDUCATION AND CARE

WHAT TEACHERS NEED TO KNOW

Why culturally responsive care and education? Children are adaptable; can't they just learn new ways of doing things? Besides, doesn't it make sense to aim to create bicultural people? Shouldn't that be a goal of education? What if parents, both immigrants and nonimmigrants, want their children to learn what they consider the "American way" and don't want their practices at home and/or their home language to be part of the school or program? These are all questions that come up in discussions of culturally responsive care and education.

Let's start with the last one first. It's true that parents may make a big separation between what goes on at home and what goes on at school or in early care and education programs. For example, at university lab schools, the foreign students who enroll their children often express a desire for their children to learn English and experience "American culture." They know their family will return to their own country, and they see the potential for their young children to go back home bilingual and with an understanding of a culture different from their own. They don't see a risk of their children losing their language or becoming alienated from their own culture.

That's a different situation from an immigrant family who has chosen to come to this country, for whatever reason, or a refugee family who ended up here but never chose to come, or a family who has been on this continent for many generations but came involuntarily, or an indigenous family who has been here for countless generations. Each of these families may have widely differing ideas about what they want for their children and what part their home language and culture should play in their child's education and development.

Imagine two families coming into a program. One has recently fled from a country where they enjoyed high socioeconomic status, and both parents are well educated. Though they are now poor, they have a different set of hopes and expectations from the second family, who arrived three generations ago, have made their living as migrant farm workers, and have children who still speak their home language. There is no way to generalize about the hopes and dreams these families have for their children without asking them. But the answers to the questions in the first paragraph may be pertinent to the separate situations described in this paragraph.

The answers to the rest of those questions fall into several themes. One is identity formation. Another is keeping connections to families strong.

The younger the child, the more unformed is his or her identity. The questions to be answered in terms of identity formation are who am I and where do I belong. According to J. Ronald Lally (1995), "Culture is the fundamental building block of identity. Through cultural learning, children gain a feeling of belonging, a sense of personal history, and security in knowing who they are and where they come from. The school or child care experience should be in harmony with the culture of the home" (p. 66). Lally wants teachers and other early childhood professionals to pay great attention to incorporating home practices into educational and care settings.

A story illustrates the identity issue. A girl named Ana entered kindergarten and proudly wrote her name for the teacher on the first day. The teacher said, "No, that's wrong, *Anna* has two n's," and the teacher corrected her spelling. Ana went home and told her mother that her name was spelled wrong. Her mother was adamant that the teacher was the one who was wrong. Ana was forced to choose between her mother and her teacher. She chose her teacher. Thirty years later, when Ana told this story, it was with tears running down her cheeks. She said the simple thing that happened in kindergarten affected the way she felt about herself, her family, and her culture. At the age of 15, she decided to reclaim her identity, but just talking about it brought more tears. Such a little thing, but such big repercussions!

Here's an example of where the teacher's goals have an effect on the child's behavior at home. A third-grade teacher is trying to get children to think for themselves. She feels the basis of a democratic society is for children to learn to question authority. To that end, she sometimes makes mistakes on purpose to see if the children will correct her. At home, however, a child in her class is taught respect for her elders, and the teacher's goals are in direct contrast to her family's. This child did fine at first, until she began bringing school behavior home. She began to question older family members, which caused a good deal of dissension in the family. Then, she began to disagree with them. The whole household was disrupted by this new behavior.

Looking at younger children, such a basic practice as feeding can be in issue. In a particular child care program, children are encouraged to practice self-help skills from early on. That means that when babies are old enough to eat finger food, they are given the chance to do so. One parent in the center has a strong reaction to arriving one day and seeing her child fingering pasta in tomato sauce and making a big mess. In this family, no one ever touches food with their fingers—even sandwiches are eaten with a knife and fork. The lessons in acceptable behavior their baby receives at the center are diametrically opposed to what the family teaches at home. Phillips and Cooper (1992) said, "Feeding has patterns of meaning that are shared by and embodied in the lifestyles of a larger group" (p. 11). So instead of explaining the importance of early self-help skills to this family, a better approach would be for the caregiver to try to understand the patterns of meaning their approaches to eating relate to. (See Strategy 17, Working with Conflicts Around Education and Care Practices.)

The teachers and caregivers in these examples need to discuss the differences in practices with family members and discuss together whether the programs should become more culturally responsive and, if so, how to do that. Such discussions might not be easy. (See Strategy 21, Managing Conflicts, for further ideas about how to proceed with the discussions.)

WHAT TEACHERS CAN DO

- Listen to what parents want for their children. Go beyond their first statements. Discuss with them the deeper aspects of their dreams and desires for their children. Ask about what the parents know about other people's experiences. Discuss biculturalism and bilingualism. You can't automatically understand a family by putting them in some broad category—like immigrant. You have to get to know them.

- Learn more about identity formation. Become aware of what messages you are sending to individual children about what is appropriate and what is inappropriate. Think about how your messages are influencing each child's sense of self, sense of cultural competence, and feelings of belonging.

- Reflect on your own early years and identity formation. How did you gain a sense of self, learn what culture you belonged to, and how well did you fit in with your family? Do you have some leftover feelings about what happened to you? Identity formation is a subject that some teachers, caregivers, and providers have never thought about before. Knowing yourself can help you better understand others.

17 WORKING WITH CONFLICTS AROUND EDUCATION AND CARE PRACTICES

WHAT TEACHERS NEED TO KNOW

Dealing with conflicts around education and care practices is a huge subject and weaves itself throughout many of the strategies in this text. Because it is impossible in a small space—or even in a lifetime—to condense all differences that can occur, this particular strategy focuses on the set of contrasting patterns mentioned in Strategy 15, patterns that influence how people see children, determine what they need, and develop educational and care practices to fit their perception and approaches.

Bridging Cultures in Early Care and Education (Zepeda, Gonzalez-Mena, Rothstein-Fisch, & Trumbull, 2006) explains the two organizing concepts, or patterns, already mentioned, which the authors call called *individualism* and *collectivism*. This particular framework is just one way in which to explore cultural and individual family differences when conflicts arise. In research done on elementary schools (Rothstein-Fisch, 2003; Trumbull, Diaz-Meza, Hasan, & Rothstein-Fisch, 2001), these concepts have been shown to be accessible and highly useful in improving home-school understanding.

When early childhood education professionals view family priorities and value systems in a non-judgmental way, they learn not only about other cultures but about their own culture as well. Culture passes from one generation to another through child-rearing practices. Culture is mostly invisible, except when it bumps up against differences in other values and belief systems through interactions. The two basic concepts—*individualism* and *collectivism*—help make visible how culture influences a person's attitudes, beliefs, values, and behaviors. Each orientation is associated with a different set of priorities that often shows up in care and education practices.

What are the differences between these two patterns? People with a strong individualistic perspective see the importance of children learning that they are unique and special individuals, so these adults stress independence and individual achievement. The focus is on the needs of the individual, self-expression, and personal choice. Physical, emotional, and mental exploration in a safe environment is often a priority. Objects become important as sources of learning about the world and how it works. Adults teach respect for personal possessions.

Although taking the individualistic perspective may seem "normal" or "natural" to you, most of the world's cultures (70% according to Triandis, 1989) and many families in North America have more collectivistic tendencies and place a higher priority on interdependence than on independence. People with a collectivistic perspective are more likely to emphasize group needs over individual needs. Social responsibility is important to people with a collectivistic orientation. They also tend to stress respect for authority and group norms. Personal possessions are downplayed, and human relationships are more important than objects.

WHAT TEACHERS CAN DO

- Remember that the concepts of individualism and collectivism are merely tools and can't be considered more than that. Don't use these tools to oversimplify or categorize people and families. It's important to refrain from stereotyping people or putting them in cultural boxes.
- Also remember that all conflicts over child-rearing differences are not cultural ones. Some may result from a family tradition, an individual experience, specific kinds of training, and philosophical ideals.

- In the face of differing ideas about early care and education practices, seek to establish common ground with individual families and groups of families without simply imposing regulations, rules, and restrictions.
- Look around to see if the program is highly individualistic: The physical environment is likely to reflect this perspective, with children having their own desks, cubbies, lockers, or coat hooks identified as "theirs" and with their names and pictures prominently displayed. Children are encouraged to take care of their property, take care of themselves (e.g., do their own work, take care of toileting, and feed and dress themselves), and use "their words" to identify their wants and needs. All of these examples are signs that individualism is valued.
- Look for the parts of the program that may reflect a more collectivistic orientation, which stresses respect for authority and obligation to group norms. In collectivistic settings, possessions are often shared, with objects being important in the context of human relationships and not in and of themselves. For instance, children may not be urged to play with objects or to investigate them independently. In a more collectivistic setting, there is more emphasis on the group than on the individual. The collectivistic perspective favors large groups for activities over small-group or individual interaction, and also mixed-aged groups where older children help and assist the younger children.
- Develop an appreciation for these contrasting patterns of care and education, and understand that they need not be mutually exclusive.
- See if you can use these two organizing concepts—individualism and collectivism—to figure out how to remain sensitive to each family's needs and wants even when they conflict with your own ideas or the program's practices.

Sometimes it looks as though people with a more collectivistic orientation "baby" people. Here is a short story about a woman who enjoyed "babying."

Roz was a family child care provider who emigrated from Taiwan to the United States as a child. Once, in a meeting of early care and education professionals, someone said it was important not to do anything for children that children could do for themselves. Roz looked skeptical and quickly said that she disagreed with that statement. She then talked about how her grandmother loved to "baby" her, even after she grew up. Roz felt it was very important that she let her grandmother take care of her, because it made the old woman happy. It didn't matter that Roz could do for herself what her grandmother did for her. Roz's response started a whole conversation as various people gave their opinions about independence and interdependence.

Jan, another family child care provider, spoke up with passion in her voice. She said that she always hated to be "babied" when she was a child—and that she hated it even more so as an adult. She said that she felt resentment toward people who didn't let her do things by herself.

Like most people, Roz and Jan don't call themselves collectivists or individualists; nevertheless, these two have very different viewpoints about being helped or helping themselves. If someone were to observe them working with children and families, it is likely that their two perspectives would have a visible influence on their behavior.

18 CONSIDERING CULTURAL DIFFERENCES IN GUIDANCE AND DISCIPLINE

WHAT TEACHERS NEED TO KNOW

In some classrooms and other early care and education programs, issues can arise around authority when the behaviors of the teacher or other adult in charge don't mirror the kinds of behaviors the child is used to at home. Images of authority are important when it comes to child guidance. For example, if the teacher takes a soft approach, using gentle words and a neutral tone of voice when correcting children, some children may ignore this teacher. If they are used to a very different tone of voice, children probably won't think that the teacher means what she says. If the teacher doesn't follow up and persist, these children may disregard rules and limits and, perhaps, become labeled as "problems." In some cases, the real problem is that the children misinterpret the meaning of what the teacher is saying. These children are used to the way that the adults in their families and extended kinship networks assert their authority at home and in the neighborhood, including stern voices, meaningful facial expressions, and strong body language, which are followed by immediate action if the words and "the look" don't work. For example, Lonnie Snowden (1984; Gonzalez-Mena, 2008a) says, "The Black community invests effective responsibility for control of children's behavior in an extensive network of adults. . . . Because of this extended parenting, children's behavior receives proper monitoring and more immediate sanctions than is the norm in American society. Children may be expected to develop more active exploratory tendencies and assertive styles, since respected external agencies can be counted on to reliably check excess" (p. 135).

When authority figures behave in ways that aren't familiar, children can feel confused (Phillips, 1995). Furthermore, some children are used to firm, strict, and sometimes even physical guidance, and without it, they keep testing the limits. They may even come to the conclusion that the teacher doesn't care what they do. These children can end up labeled as "problem children" (Hale-Benson, 1986).

It's important to note that firm limits actually give some children more freedom, because children then know that somebody will stop them if they go too far. When the teacher just talks and doesn't stop them, they continue to push to find out what the limits are. Children don't recognize that they are getting guidance and direction from the adults in that situation, but that those adults aren't like the ones at home. Instead of being strict and insisting on certain behaviors, these adults are stressing individual choice. The lessons then come from the children living with the consequences of their actions. They don't scold or threaten. They don't punish. They allow natural consequences within reason— ones that don't harm the child but that may feel uncomfortable. When there are no natural consequences, they set up the situation so that there are logical consequences (Dreikurs, 1990). The adult can do this without even changing facial expression or tone of voice. This can all be done in a matter-of-fact manner.

Cynthia Ballenger (1992) writes about the problem of children's confusion over adults' authority when Haitian children encounter teachers who stress individual choice and living with the consequences of that choice. The Haitian teachers didn't think in terms of individual choice but, rather, in defined behavior as either good and bad. They warned children that bad behavior would bring shame on the family. They told the children that they had a responsibility to be good and scolded them when they weren't good. The teachers regarded reprimands as ways to strengthen the relationship and show children that someone cared about them and their behavior. That is a contrast to more neutral approaches that avoid reprimands, allow children to make choices to discover what the consequences are, and put responsibility on the individual.

We don't know if this teacher's style matches the style of the child's parents, but she does look like she means business, even if she is being gentle about it.

So how do you work with parents around differences in how children are expected to relate to authority?

WHAT TEACHERS CAN DO

- When the teacher acts one way and the family another, this situation calls for some serious discussion. If you already have a relationship with the parent and there is mutual trust, it will be easier to talk about how to help the child get along both at school and at home.
- Start by observing the parent with the child, and suspend judgment if the parent's behavior doesn't match what you think is the right approach to guidance and discipline.
- Have the parent observe how you handle misbehavior, and talk about it afterward.
- If there is a drastic difference, expect the dilemma to be resolved eventually, but probably not right away. Try to learn about the parent's approach, the reasons behind it, and the expected outcomes. If this is a cross-cultural situation, you may both have something to learn about the other person's cultural differences.
- Explain your approach and why you do what you do, but don't try to sell it to the parent. This should be a mutual exchange of information.
- Continue to work on the relationship.
- Try different approaches with the child if the ones you use don't work and the ones the parents use do. That doesn't mean you have to give up your own values or imitate the parent. By all means, don't do anything you perceive as harmful to the child.
- Open your mind to the idea that what you see as harmful may not be in the context of the family or their culture. For example, if you are trained in the principles of early childhood education, you won't use name calling as a way to guide behavior, because in general, such a practice is regarded as detrimental to children's self-image. If parents call children a name or use some kind of label, you can't judge what that name or label means to the child, especially if it is a cross-cultural situation and in a language you don't speak.

19 WORKING WITH FAMILIES AROUND WHAT YOU BELIEVE ARE HARMFUL PRACTICES

WHAT TEACHERS NEED TO KNOW

A difficult situation arises when the early childhood professional finds out that what the family is doing is harmful to the child. If abuse or neglect is suspected, the professional must report it to the authorities. (See Strategy 50, Referring Families for Abuse or Neglect.) A behavior or practice that doesn't fit the legal definition of abuse is a different matter. This is a delicate situation and must be handled sensitively. If you confront the family member with accusations, you may destroy the relationship that you have been building. If you ignore the situation, the child may suffer.

Take the example of a first-grade teacher whose student says that her mother spanked her that morning on her legs. This teacher feels strongly that spanking is harmful, but there are no bruises or even red marks on the child's legs. The teacher knows that spanking is legal as long as there are no lasting marks. She is concerned about this child and this family, but as she gets to know them better, she discovers that spanking is the only method they know for guiding their children. If the teacher managed to talk them out of using spanking as a disciplinary measure without giving them some other ideas of strategies that make sense to them, the family would be left without any way to guide their children's behavior. That would be a grave disservice to the family. So instead, the teacher started a series of discussion groups on discipline, which were very popular and widely attended! All the parents who came, including the one mother who concerned the teacher, seemed to get a great deal out of the sessions.

Here's another example of a potentially harmful practice. A grandmother enrolls her three-month-old granddaughter in your infant center and tells you that she is to be put to sleep on her stomach. When you hesitate, she insists that the baby can't sleep on her back. Besides, it's dangerous, she says, because the baby may spit up and choke. You think the grandmother is just old-fashioned or uninformed. But then she plays the cultural card and tells you that it is a tradition in her culture for babies to sleep on their tummies. Should you be culturally responsive and go along with her, or will you argue that babies on their tummies are at risk for SIDS (Sudden Infant Death Syndrome)?

It will help both the baby and your relationship with the family if you seek to understand more about the grandmother's ideas and cultural traditions. It's important to recognize that in some cultures, SIDS is less of a risk than in others, especially if babies never sleep alone. Cosleeping is common practice among many families. Also, regardless of culture, certain medical conditions put babies in more danger when on their backs. That is not to say that you should automatically go along with what the grandmother says. You would be professionally remiss if you didn't share at least your understanding of the research that indicates babies are at greater risk for SIDS when sleeping on their stomachs. Statistics may not impress her, but try to state things in terms she might listen to. Don't argue with her. Share your information in an open way, and ask her more about her point of view. It might help to find out if this is a common belief of her culture, or if some members of her culture (or even her own family) have a different view of stomach sleeping. After all, it wasn't even a generation ago that everybody in the United States who followed medical advice placed their babies to sleep on their stomachs because it was considered safer than back sleeping.

A cultural practice that may startle teachers, caregivers, and providers is something called "coining," a healing or preventative practice of some people in various Asian cultures, which involves putting a special liquid on the skin and then rubbing a coin or a spoon on the area. The rubbing is hard enough to leave lasting red marks and, unless you understand it, may appear to be an abusive practice.

One person's approved healing or preventative practice may seem abusive to someone who doesn't understand it. For example, think of immunization. If people had no idea about immunization, what would they think of a parent letting someone stick a needle in his baby's arm? The parent might explain to the doubters that this is a preventative measure and that it doesn't harm the baby. But the observers might not believe it, especially if the baby cried in pain at the shot—and especially if she got sick later on. Unless the observers were from a culture that believed in science and could accept the technical explanation of the procedure, they would have to take on faith that this was, indeed, a preventative measure, because they saw with their own eyes that it hurt the baby and made her ill. What would it take for someone who knew nothing about Western science or medicine to understand? What would it take for you to understand a healing or protection practice that was contradictory to Western science or medicine? We all need to be open to the idea that our way isn't the only right way.

WHAT TEACHERS CAN DO

- Don't judge immediately. Seek to understand more. Barbara Rogoff (2003) suggests that even though judgments may be necessary, we can make better decisions when we do judge if we can move beyond the idea that our ideas are the only right ones. Only when we can see a situation in context and understand perspectives, ideas, and beliefs other than our own can we make wise judgments. (See Strategy 17, Working with Conflicts Around Education and Care Practices, and Strategy 21, Managing Conflicts.)

- At the same time that you are making sure not to judge too quickly, don't hesitate to report abuse when it meets the legal definition of your state. Too often children die while the people who could have saved them held off reporting suspected abuse.

- In all events, try to preserve whatever relationship you have managed to build with the family.

- Work on your listening skills. Using imagination helps, too, as you try to see things from a perspective not your own. Try what Betty Jones and Renatta Cooper (2006) call "the believing game." They say, "Imagining another person's perspective on things requires the suspension of reality (what I really believe) in order to pretend. (This is what someone else believes. Could I, if I tried hard?) In the diverse world we live in, we keep encountering people who don't believe what we believe. We can sneer at them, or fight them, or pretend they're invisible (until they step on our toe). Or we can accept the challenge to 'embrace contraries'" (p. 23).

- Find people from diverse backgrounds with whom you can have discussions. Then, ask questions, and learn more.

20 THINKING ABOUT DIFFERING IDEAS RELATED TO HOW CHILDREN LEARN

WHAT TEACHERS NEED TO KNOW

Parents remember their own education when they judge the classroom or program their child is in. If parents were taught to sit up straight at a desk, they may be critical of a classroom with tables and chairs and, maybe, a reading corner that has cushions on the floor. If, on the other hand, they enjoyed an early educational experience like the historic Summerhill School, where play was part of the curriculum and children made decisions about what they wanted to do and where they wanted to do it (indoors or outside), parents may frown at their children having to sit at desks in order to learn.

Readiness issues can be on many parents' minds when they enter early childhood programs. Obviously, families want their children to do well in school, so they may want a strong push for academics in kindergarten and first grade beyond what research shows is developmentally appropriate (Copple and Bredekamp, 2009).

Parent's ideas about what should happen before kindergarten can vary greatly. Early childhood educators who work with children under 5 may also have varied opinions about this subject, but those who have been trained in early childhood principles and practices are likely to have a developmental view. They probably see play as part of the curriculum, a view that not all parents share. Thus, conflicts can arise. It's not unusual for a family or a group of families to push the preschool teacher for early academics, hoping that their children will be reading before kindergarten. When professionals argue the perspective of developmental appropriateness, they may convince some families, but others will dig in harder in order to push their point of view.

Sometimes the family's ideas come from messages they hear that are based on misinterpretations of brain development research. The pressure for early academics is strong from all sides.

Sometimes ideas about teaching academics arise from cultural differences rather than misunderstandings about brain research. For example, a Chinese mother's own experience in learning to read in her native language influenced her ideas about how children should learn to read in English, even though learning characters takes different skills than learning to read in a language that uses an alphabet. She thought her child should be sitting down and memorizing words instead of playing with play dough and finger paint at preschool. Instead of arguing with this mother, the child's teacher listened to what she had to say, even if the teacher didn't agree with her about what was best for the child at this stage of development. Staying away from arguing created more of a partnership atmosphere, and the mother and teacher eventually became collaborators instead of adversaries.

One prerequisite for entering a dialogue is for early childhood education professionals to explore their own attitudes toward particular parents or parents in general. (See Strategy 7, Removing Barriers to Partnership.) They should do some soul searching about what they truly believe and explore emotional hotspots that can get in the way of good listening. It is also useful if they can become articulate about the program's policy on readiness so that they can explain it to parents who have a different idea without coming on too strong and without arguing. If professionals believe in the policy, they can put aside their defensiveness and learn about a different perspective from their own. Thus, the people in question can create a useful dialogue. Once they have heard each other enough so that they have a bigger picture than originally, maybe they can stop taking sides and begin to figure out what is best for this child, or a particular group of children, in this setting.

This is one of the many situations where good listening skills are necessary. Professionals need to make sure families feel that they are heard. They also need to work hard to understand just what it is

Notice how this setting for play is in a print-rich environment. One aspect of readiness is what is called early literacy, which involves books and beginning letter recognition.

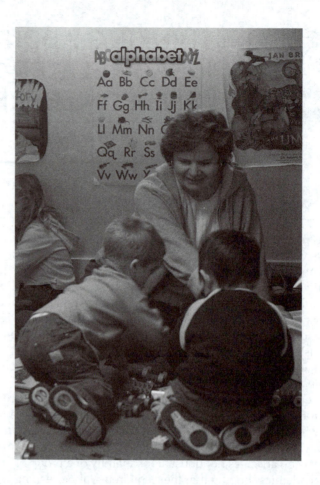

that families want. If after some dialoguing there is still disagreement, conflict resolution or consensus building skills are needed. (See Strategy 21, Managing Conflicts.) Be sure that any process toward resolution builds the relationship instead of tearing it down.

Getting children excited about learning is a goal common to most early childhood programs. Sharing that goal with parents can be useful. The joy of learning comes when children are encouraged to become creative, competent explorers and problem solvers. Play and exploration may not look like educational activities to some parents, but when they understand that their children are learning how to learn, they may come to appreciate the approach as useful.

WHAT TEACHERS CAN DO

- Regard a child's exploratory tendencies as an important learning skill. In the preschool years, but even in kindergarten and the primary grades, those tendencies still lead children down the path to learning. Teachers of the K-3 level can provide for exploration by using manipulative materials in math lessons, for example. Exploration may look more physical than mental, especially in very young children, yet those same qualities are what inventors, discoverers, and creators throughout history have used to add to the body of knowledge that exists today. How many explorers go straight to their goal? Not many. Amazing things are discovered while meandering.
- Hone your observation skills, and help parents hone theirs so that the value they put on play is increased when they observe what their children are learning as they play. Parents may even come to see the benefits of allowing free play for longer periods (rather than regarding it as recess—a time to rest from learning). When adults understand how capable most children are of rich, creative play, they may interrupt it less and step back so that they don't direct or take over.

- Model resourcefulness yourself so that children see you as a learner. When children ask why, work with them to find the answer. Furthermore, let parents know what you are doing, and invite them to be part of the process.

- Help parents see how they can use encouragement rather than praise so that children are more likely to regard learning as its own reward and depend less on adult recognition of success. Help parents understand the benefits of emphasizing intrinsic rewards that come from the inside by saying, "You must feel so good about what you just accomplished there." Extrinsic rewards are rewards from the outside and make children dependent on somebody else for motivation to learn. Extrinsic rewards can be social rewards—praise or something tangible, like a piece of candy. Use these kinds of devices, even star charts, sparingly, and don't set up competitions to see who gets the most rewards.

- Don't argue about any of the preceding suggestions. Become aware of the difference between an argument and a dialogue. The purpose of a dialogue is to understand—not to win. The idea is to expand one's knowledge rather than trying to persuade the other person to accept a different point of view.

- Instead of arguing, offer families opportunities to observe you with their children, and then model what you believe in. The idea is not to win the family over but, rather, to expand their views—just as your goal should be to expand your own views through observation of families with their children as well as ongoing dialogue with the family.

- When creating a dialogue, remember that communication involves listening as well as talking. Sometimes we have to listen twice as much as we talk if we are to gain a bigger picture and a deeper understanding.

Families have differing ideas about how children learn—some think they should be active, and others think they should sit at desks and concentrate on seat work. Even the room arrangement can be a point of contention. Every family might not agree about this classroom setup, where children's desks are together at different angles instead of in rows facing the teacher's desk.

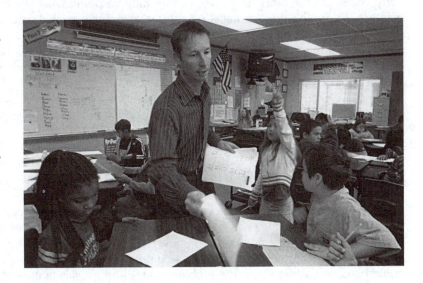

21 MANAGING CONFLICTS

WHAT TEACHERS NEED TO KNOW

Though the long-term goal of conflict management is to resolve the disagreement, the immediate and ongoing goal should be to keep from destroying the relationship while trying to reach consensus. The key to both goals is effective communication. Communication is a huge subject and has its own section as well as being woven throughout this book. This particular strategy is aimed at seeing how to take two seemingly opposite points of view and figuring out what to do that will work for everybody. An approach taken by Barrera and Corso (2003), a professor of special education at the University of New Mexico, involves what she calls *third space*.

Third space has to do with moving from dualistic thinking to holistic thinking in the face of what seems to be a contradiction or a paradox. If a parent whose child has been in preschool where children learn mostly through play arrives in kindergarten to see children sitting at desks with seat work, it's possible that she and the teacher have very different concepts about what children need in their early years. On the other hand, the teacher may be doing what she has to do rather than what she wants to do. For this discussion, let's say this teacher believes that seat work is important way that children learn and that play is not.

Here's another example from an infant-toddler program. Say a parent starts toilet training her baby at six months of age and the policy of the center is to wait until after the second birthday. That situation can create a conflict.

In these examples, both parties have reasons for what they are doing. The teacher in the first and caregiver in the second may think "I'm right, and she's wrong." The parents in both examples may think the opposite of the teacher and caregiver.

If arguments start, it's likely that the school or the center will win if the parent perceives the power to be in other hands—especially if policy, research, or experts are quoted, which can tip the balance in favor of the school or center. However, parents who lose arguments probably won't feel like partners with their child's teacher or caregiver.

Aiming for third-space solutions means that conflicts move beyond winning and losing, relationships flourish, and nobody has to give in. The idea of everybody winning in the face of a conflict flies in the face of logic for many Western thinkers, who are used to competitive situations in which there is always a loser. Another factor that can get in the way of reaching a third-space solution is what could be called a *blind spot*. The problem with blind spots is that we don't know we have them. As I once said to a friend who has tunnel vision, "So is it like looking through two paper towel tubes and everything else is black?" He laughed and said to me, "Janet, what I don't see out of the corners of my eyes is exactly like what you don't see out of the back of your head!" My friend has a blind spot and so do I, but I never think about it.

What does tunnel vision have to do with this conflict over play versus seat work or toilet training? Let's say that the teacher thinks seat work is very important for children's success in school. She has the principal's support and district policy to back her up. When faced with a parent who wants play in the classroom, she may feel she's right and the parent's wrong. In the caregiver's case, let's say that the caregiver has knowledge and experience when it comes to toilet training and has had a hand in setting the program's policy. She is confident in her approach. When faced with a parent whose ideas clash with her expertise and program policy, she judges the parent to be wrong, because she has a blind spot that she is unaware of. She is missing a whole piece of what toilet training means to this parent, just as the teacher in the first example doesn't know what play means to that parent. Both professionals consider the parents' approaches to be a *problem*.

If told the conflict should end in a win-win solution, both of these professionals would feel stuck in the face of a paradox. How can they solve this problem? To be culturally or individually sensitive, do they have to give in to something they believe is unrealistic, wrong, or even harmful?

No! Barbara Rogoff (2003) says, "Understanding different cultural practices does not require determining which one way is 'right' (which does not mean that all ways are fine). With an understanding of what is done in different circumstances, we can be open to possibilities that do not necessarily exclude each other" (p. 14). Often when faced with a dilemma, the teacher who is trying hard to be culturally responsive may just give in when he begins to see a cultural view that's different from his own. But you don't have to give up your own ways when you learn about cultural differences. Instead, put assumptions aside, and seek to understand rather than judge. You can make some guesses as to what cultural patterns are represented in such a situation, but you may not be right. Rogoff recommends that you continually test and revise your ideas. As she reminds us, "*There's always more to learn*" (p. 14).

It is possible that the teacher and the parent are closer in their ideas than they think. If they didn't put themselves on opposite sides, they might be surprised at what they can come up with. In the toilet training example, the parent's ideas likely are related to cultural or family traditions and have patterns of meaning that the caregiver doesn't understand. (See Strategy 17 for examples of differing patterns of meaning.) Knowing that there are reasons for what the parent is doing that are valid in her mind, however, may still not bring comfort to the caregiver when facing the paradox of two seemingly incompatible approaches.

Parker Palmer (1997) gives advice about how to look at the positive side of paradox. He writes: "We split paradoxes so reflexively that we do not understand the price we pay for our habit. The poles of a paradox are like the poles of a battery: hold them together, and they generate the energy of life; pull them apart, and the current stops flowing. When we separate any of the profound paired truths of our lives, both poles become lifeless as well. Dissecting a living paradox has the same impact on our intellectual, emotional, and spiritual well-being as the decision to breathe in without ever breathing out would have on our physical health" (p. 64).

"Paired truths" is a useful term when working to see a paradox as positive, but that concept may be difficult to understand when the people in conflict see themselves as on opposite sides. They still have to figure out what to do.

Barrera and Corso (2003) give some insight into how to use third space in this situation. "A third space perspective does not 'solve the problem.' Rather it changes the arena within which that problem is addressed by increasing the probability of respectful, responsive, and reciprocal interactions. In so doing, an optimal response to the situation becomes more likely" (p. 81).

One way to enter that area is to move from dualistic thinking to holistic thinking. In dualistic thinking, contrasting ideas are looked at as dichotomous, which gets in the way of trying to solve problems. If it's right, it can't be wrong. If it's bad, it can't be good. If it's blue, it can't be yellow. When you move into holistic thinking from dualistic thinking, you don't separate differences into opposites. An example of holistic thinking is to bring blue and yellow together to make green! Blue keeps its blueness and yellow keeps its yellowness, and together, they make something new altogether. Green is an example of third space.

Bredekamp and Copple (1997) explained third space without naming it in the second edition of *Developmentally Appropriate Practice in Early Childhood Programs* published by the National Association for the Education of Young Children (NAEYC). They said, "Some critical reactions to NAEYC's (1997) position statement on developmentally appropriate practice reflect a recurring tendency in the American discourse on education: the polarizing into *either/or* choices of many questions that are more fruitfully seen as *both/and*" (p. 23). In the new edition of that same book, they integrate both/and perspectives throughout (Copple & Bredekamp, 2009).

WHAT TEACHERS CAN DO

- The first step in working toward consensus around an area of conflict is to suspend judgment and try to understand the other person's perspective. Barbara Rogoff (2003) writes: "We must separate *understanding of patterns from judgments of their value*. If judgments of value are necessary, as they often are, they will thereby be much better informed if they are suspended long enough to gain some understanding of the patterns involved in one's own familiar ways as well as in the sometimes surprising ways of other communities" (p. 14). (See Strategies 15 and 17 about patterns.)

- To suspend judgment, take the advice of Rumi, a 13th century poet, who wrote: "Out beyond ideas of wrongdoing and rightdoing there lies a field. I will meet you there." If you go out to that field with a parent to talk about your views, you may be able to see a reality that is bigger than both of you.

- Appreciate the energy of paired truths, and remember that according to Parker Palmer (1997), only adhering to one of them is like breathing in without breathing out. Instead of trying to solve the problem right away, go out to Rumi's field, which changes the arena in which you can have a dialogue and gives you a chance to engage in holistic thinking.

- Seek an optimal response to the situation, and at the same time, increase the depth and strength of the relationship. This approach makes it easier to figure out what to do about your differences in this situation with this child and family in this classroom or program. In his foreword to *Crucial Conversations*, Steven Covey (2002) uses the term *synergy* to label third space. He says it is imperative that we nourish our relationships and develop tools, skills, and enhanced capacity to find new and better solutions to our problems. These newer, better solutions will not represent "my way" or "your way"—they will represent "our way."

The first step in working toward consensus when conflict surfaces is to suspend judgment and try to understand the other person's perspective. Is that what the woman with the glasses in her hand is doing? Maybe.

- Recognize that to reach a third-space or synergistic solution you need to:
  - Believe it possible.
  - Accept that there are multiple realities and paired truths.
  - Change from arguing and persuading to dialoguing.
- Practice using dialoguing instead of arguing, because according to Steven Covey, genuine dialogue "*transforms* people and relationships . . . and creates an entirely new level of bonding producing what Buddhism calls 'the middle way'—not a compromise between two opposites on a straight-line continuum, but a higher middle way, like the apex of a triangle" (p. xii)

Once, in a workshop, the issue of differences in ideas about toilet training came up. I said, "You don't have to do what the parent wants. It's hard in a center, and I'm just telling you to be respectful of the difference." As I finished the sentence, a hand shot up from the audience. A participant was obviously very eager to speak. She stood up and said, "Here's what happened to me. A mother brought her one-year-old daughter to the center for the first time, and she told me that she was already toilet trained. I didn't believe her, but instead of responding negatively, I asked her to show me what she did. She showed me and it worked! The baby was trained and didn't need to wear diapers. It didn't take any more time and energy than changing diapers would have." What surprised me about this story was that the participant, though willing to try something new, really didn't have faith that it would work. She was wrong. It did work. This story illustrates a win-win solution. The caregiver kept on with what she believed in for the other children but was also able to satisfy the mother. In other words, the caregiver expanded her ideas about what was possible and didn't give up anything.

22 CONSIDERING FAMILY PARTICIPATION

WHAT TEACHERS NEED TO KNOW

Sometimes called "parent involvement," family participation in schools, preschools, infant-toddler programs, and other early childhood programs can include anything from assisting in the classroom to serving on a board or advisory committee to building furniture. Other parent involvement activities can include taking equipment home to repair, washing paint smocks, contributing supplies, or coming in on a Saturday to spruce up the yard. Attending parent education sessions is yet another example of family participation. Fund-raising is still another way that families can participate.

Cooperative preschools are one example of parent participation programs and are built on parent involvement. They have been influential in getting parents whose children move on to kindergarten and the primary grades into the classrooms of their children. Without their influence, the old tradition of separating home and school would still be in effect, such as when parents sent their children off to the teachers in their classroom and neither side crossed the threshold of the other.

Traditionally, cooperative preschools have focused more on the whole of development rather than the more narrow view of school readiness or academics. That influence has brought developmentally appropriate practice into an increasing number of schools as teachers come to understand a broader definition of "readiness."

Many of the parent participation programs are sponsored by public school districts or linked with an adult education program. Often the parents run the program, hire the teacher, and/or sit on the decision-making board. Enrolled families usually are required to have a parent work in the classroom on a regular, weekly basis. Sometimes the participating parents for that day meet after the session is over to discuss what happened. Generally, the programs have children for only half a day. These after-the-session meetings are part of the parent education arm of the program and are often coupled with night meetings for the whole group. Parents who have the time and interest to be deeply involved with their children's care and education are the ones who choose this type of program.

If the family is sending the child to public school and/or to child care while they work, required parent involvement may not be what the family wants or has time for. One of the themes of this book is to create partnerships with parents, so it's important to mention that mandated parent involvement can work against the partnership. If one program goal is empowerment, then requiring families to do something they don't want to or don't have time for works in opposition to that goal. Anyone who is truly interested in developing partnerships with parents needs to think about how to use parent involvement toward that end rather than in a way that defeats it.

Joyce Epstein (2001), director of the National Network of Partnership Schools, breaks parent involvement into six categories of activities used by schools:

1. Parent-education activities
2. Communications between schools and families
3. Volunteer opportunities
4. At-home learning activities
5. Decision-making opportunities
6. Community collaborations

Family participation and parent involvement are behind the concept that success for the child is linked to families becoming part of the child's care and education program. Success may be defined as academic achievement, school readiness, enhanced learning, or optimal development of the whole child.

WHAT TEACHERS CAN DO

- Start by making parents and other family members feel comfortable and welcome, both when they enter the program and on a continuing basis.
- Set up an environment that says to family members, "You belong here." If possible, make a welcoming space for them. In preschool programs, it may be easier to include such things as a place for family members to sit, toys for younger siblings, and a bulletin board with items of interest for parents. Some classrooms and programs have mailboxes for each family, pamphlets available, and even books to lend. A steaming coffee pot out of the reach of little hands is an added bonus.
- An open-door policy lets families know that their presence is always welcome, though that may be difficult in K-3 classrooms.
- Work to develop a relationship with each family member who comes into the program. In preschools and infant-toddler programs, just being available when the child arrives or is picked up is a good beginning for a relationship.
- Find out what interests the family has, and ask how the program can serve them better. This is a good policy for programs that serve children of all ages. When the family is also a focus instead of just the child, programs can provide or organize activities that families really want to participate in, such as excursions, parties, and Friday night pizza and video for the whole family. After this policy gets going, a parent committee can take over the planning and organizing.
- Suggest ways family members can help out or become part of the program. This works best after you get to know the family and understand their strengths, interests, and skills.
- Offer opportunities to observe. This can be a start for parents in getting to know the program and figuring out where they best fit in as participating family members.
- Help each family get to know other families in the program.
- If parents are willing to give out contact information, create an address list to pass out.
- Notice which children spend time with each other, and tell the parents of both, in case they want to make play dates.

This cooperative preschool and kindergarten brochure states that the program is child-centered but the parents own the school, so there is a constant family presence in all aspects of its operation. The parent's role is spelled out in this brochure.

Notes of appreciation are a good way to keep parents and other family members volunteering in the classroom.

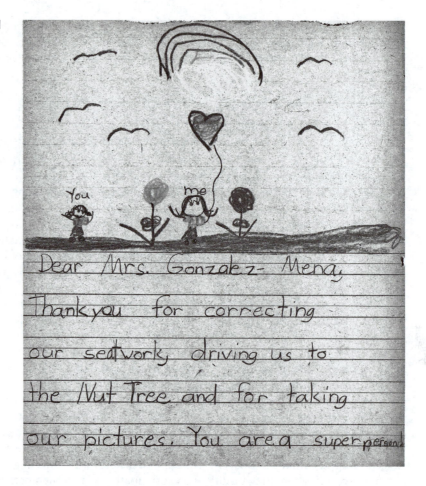

Dear Mrs. Gonzalez-Mena,
Thankyou for correcting our seatwork, driving us to the Nut Tree and for taking our pictures. You are a superperson!

- Look for barriers that may be keeping some families from participating, and see which ones you can eliminate. Can younger siblings come along with the parent who wants to spend time in the classroom? Can an occasional Saturday event help the parents who want to be involved but are busy on weekdays?
- Recognize that some families see school as separate and apart from family life, and they expect teachers to do the educating without involving them. The whole idea of parent involvement may be very strange to them, and parents may feel inadequate to see themselves as their "child's first teacher." Don't push them to do things they feel uncomfortable doing. Just keep working on building a relationship with them.

A story about family participation: One family felt so at home in their child care center that when the child went into kindergarten, the family welcomed the list of ways to participate that the teacher handed out the first day. This family became the catalyst for other families who weren't used to participating in their children's programs.

This family is a contrast to a family who came into the child care center with the idea that this was school and the teacher was the one who knew about education. They had great respect for this teacher—and any teacher—so they put her on a pedestal. Their attitude influenced their relationship with her. When this family met another family from their same culture who had a different idea about the child care center, they began to see a different perspective. The family they met had a cousin who was an assistant teacher in the program, and she helped them feel right at home in the center. Then, they began to notice how involved their new friends were in the program, and that gave them the idea they could be involved too. Eventually, they started looking for ways to help out. One day, the grandmother offered to take home the paint smocks to wash over the weekend. When she brought the smocks back on Monday, she noticed a father reading a book in Spanish to a small group of children. That gave her the idea to offer to teach the children some songs and finger plays from her own

Family participation and parent involvement have been around for a long time at all kinds of early childhood programs for children from birth through age 8. One idea behind the concept is that success for the child is linked to families becoming part of their children's care and education program.

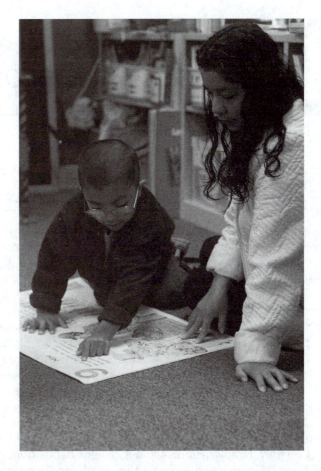

childhood. Later, the mother offered to come in and make tortillas with the children. While she was there, she got the idea that maybe the center could have a potluck evening, when each family could bring an ethnic dish to share. What started as no involvement ended up as plenty of involvement, and none of it was required.

23 INCLUDING PARENTS IN THE CLASSROOM OR CENTER

WHAT TEACHERS NEED TO KNOW

Strategy 22 looked at family participation from an overall view. This one zeros in on how to use family members as volunteers in the classroom, which is a common way of getting them involved in their children's education. Head Start has used this strategy successfully since it started in the mid-sixties. Some K-3 classrooms as well as other preschool and infant-toddler programs also utilize parent volunteers, but not all of them do. For some programs, it is mandated; for others, it's not. There are many models for parent volunteers. Some cooperative preschools depend on parents as teachers to fill out adult to child ratios. Whether kindergarten and primary teachers use parent volunteers depends on many factors, including district policies and regulations, specialized funding, school traditions, and the teachers' own inclinations.

Having parents in the center or classroom works well when early childhood professionals are dedicated to families and view their job as family-centered care and education. It doesn't work as well when these professionals come into the field because they like working with children but dislike working with parents. In some cases, this is an early stage of professional development—the focus on children and disregard of parents—but in other cases, this attitude remains throughout the career of the professional.

Certainly, family members in the center or classroom complicate the job of the professional. For one thing, it increases the number of people and interactions. The teacher, staff, or caregiver must plan for the extra adults as well as for the children. Children can behave very differently in the presence of their parents, which can disrupt the group.

Advocates for parents in the center or classroom cite many advantages. Family members who spend time being involved in their children's education find out about what goes on in the classroom and see how their children learn. For many parents, their experience as an early learner occurred in a more highly structured, strict, academic environment, and spending time in their own child's center or classroom helps them to understand developmental processes and the special approaches that work for children in their beginning years. Family members in the classroom can observe firsthand the ways their children interact with others. It broadens their view of their own children. For some parents, being involved in the classroom is an eye-opening experience as they learn more about typical development.

Volunteering in the center or classroom makes parents and other family members feel good to be able to contribute to the program. The more time they spend there, the more ideas they come up with about how they can use their own talents, skills, and interests to make unique contributions. When they see how other parents bring in cultural artifacts and activities, that idea spreads.

Feelings of security on the part of the parents and their children increase when parents spend time in the classroom or center. The relationships between families and staff can solidify as they get to know each other better than just the quick, daily hellos and good-byes and scattered meetings throughout the year.

WHAT TEACHERS CAN DO

- Consider instituting an open-door policy that encourages parents and other family members to feel free to visit the center or classroom at any time. For some professionals, a more specific visiting time may work better—for example, one afternoon a week, family members are invited to come early and visit before their children go home.

Parent volunteers come into the classroom to take dictation as children learn that what they say can be represented in written words. This was an October activity and represents a story by Timmy about a pumpkin. Later, he copied the story himself on another piece of paper.

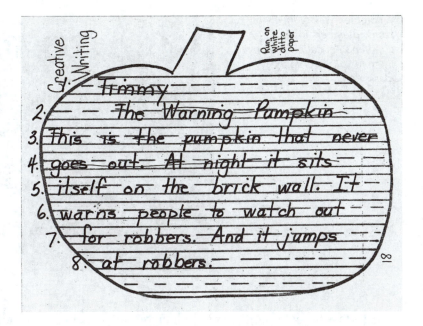

Preschoolers get more personal attention when parent volunteers are in the center encouraging the children to get involved in the various activities set out for them. A parent volunteer helped with this art project.

- If parents and other family members are coming into the classroom to assist the teacher or caregiver, it makes those family members feel more secure if there is some kind of training they can receive—either formal or informal.
- Informal training takes into consideration what beginners need to know right away. Certainly, they need to know the expectations of the professional and the routine of the classroom. They need a description of what they are to do and instructions or tips about how to do it. Some of these things they can learn over time, but they need definite instructions for their first day. A day of observation before they begin to actually help out can give them an idea of how things work.

A common way of involving family members in their children's education is to invite them to volunteer in the classroom.

- A formal training program could include the specifics provided by informal training plus a broader overview of the field, such as an orientation to the principles, practices, and goals that relate to early childhood philosophy. Developmental information can be useful as well, plus some ideas about learning styles and how to respond to individual children as well as groups. Some tips on guidance approaches will help the parents understand what the professional is doing and make them feel more secure when they are faced with the need to guide behavior into positive routes.

- Invite parents to observe. This is a very different role from helping out, and it needs to be explained to everybody—children as well as parents. It helps if there is a special badge to wear, a certain chair to sit in, or some other way of signaling that the family member is in an observation mode so that everybody understands what to expect.

- Consider other possibilities of parents in the classroom or center besides using them as helpers, assistant teachers, or observers. They can help plan and carry out special social events for special occasions or for birthdays. Before instituting this idea, though, be sure that all families are okay with celebrations. Some families, for religious reasons, cannot participate in such events. Be sensitive to differences and honor them. (See Strategy 26, Working with Parents Around Holiday Issues.) A different way of bringing parents into the classroom is what one first-grade teacher does. She has parents come in twice a week for half an hour, first thing in the morning, to read to and with their children. Many of those who show up are fathers.

24 FOCUSING ON FATHERS

WHAT TEACHERS NEED TO KNOW

Fathers aren't all the same. Just as there are all kinds of mothers in all kinds of situations, the same is true for fathers. Some fathers live with the mother and their children and are closely connected; others live in the same house but are not so closely connected. Some fathers live with the other father rather than the mother. In any family, there may be blood ties or not. There may be marriage ties or not. Some fathers live with their children as single parents. Some fathers are raising their stepchildren as single parents. It's very hard to make a generalized statement about fathers except to say that some early childhood education programs have a harder time involving men than they do women.

One group of fathers that may not get enough attention from early childhood professionals are those who don't live with their children. Parent Services Project (mentioned in Strategy 14, Creating a Sense of Community) created a fatherhood project aimed at involving fathers who are not living with their children. A goal of the project was to give these fathers the support they needed to have positive relationships with their children. Some of them who never had affection in their own childhood learned how to give it to their children, and they reaped the rewards of that behavioral change. The project put on workshops in parenting, which included communication and conflict resolution. The fathers also learned about stress management and financial management, as well receiving job training. The outcomes of that project were remarkable and included fewer child behavior problems, higher levels of sociability, and even a reduction in childhood poverty. Some of the fathers in this project turned their lives around, making changes that benefited themselves, their children, and their communities. As they got involved in school and other early care and education programs, they learned the importance of making time for their children.

James Levine (1993a) saw four barriers to getting men involved in Head Start and public preschool programs:

1. Father's fear of exposing inadequacies
2. Ambivalence of program staff members about father involvement
3. Gatekeeping by mothers
4. Inappropriate program design and delivery

When programs are designed for involvement by the mother rather than including both parents, men can feel uncomfortable and unwelcome. Some hints that this is happening come when teachers tend to talk to the mothers, not the fathers; when conferences are held at times when few fathers can attend; when no men work in the program; and when a child lives in two homes but only one set of newsletters and notices are sent out.

Some men arrive in K-3 classrooms and other early childhood education programs already involved in their children's lives. They've had experience in the PTA or other parent-teacher organizations as members or officers. Some have been involved with Little League as coaches. Many children enter kindergarten from Head Start, where both their parents were involved. Those experienced fathers sometimes are more easily able to involve other fathers than are the teachers or staff in the program. If you can get them organized to reach out to other men, the rate of male involvement can go up.

To get men involved in most programs, the staff has to be intentional about it. Leaving male involvement to chance almost always means that many more mothers will be involved than fathers.

Stanley Seiderman, director of the Bay Area Male Involvement Network in California, had good ideas about how to make involvement in early care and education programs more attractive to men. He said, "The strongest motivators for getting and keeping fathers involved in all aspects of their child's life are expectation, encouragement and opportunity. While it is true that there are men who want to get involved and need little help to do so, most men will not usually come forward in our child care settings. They tend to be reticent and uncomfortable" (Lee, 2004).

WHAT TEACHERS CAN DO

- Make all fathers feel welcome. Go back and look at Strategy 4 about creating an antibias environment. Read through each strategy, keeping a focus on fathers. Analyze an early care and education environment in terms of fathers while keeping those strategies in mind. If you were a father, what would welcome you? What would feel less than inviting?
- Figure out how to get more male teachers and staff members. Explore the barriers to males entering the field, and begin to address them. (See Strategy 13 on advocacy.)
- Recognize that males experience the world differently from the way that females do. Though early childhood professionals may have a strong value of gender equity, we still have to acknowledge that being a male is different from being a female. We might even see those differences in terms of cultural ones.
- Learn more about the differences in male and female experiences by observation and discussion. One way to learn more is to increase the number of male teachers and staff members so that the numbers are more even.
- Don't assume that what you know about the differences in male and female experiences are universal. Each culture varies in what males experience and what females experience. There is plenty to learn.
- Recognize that the field of early education and care in schools and other settings has its own culture, and that those of us who have training and experience in the field have become part of it, though we may not even be aware of the idea of it being a *culture*. Female influences have created this culture (consciously and unconsciously) more than male influences have. This is a huge emotional subject and could be debated at length.
- Learn more about the culture of early childhood education by observation and discussion. The more the this culture is talked about, the more aware we will all become of it.

Children benefit when their fathers are part of the early care and education program. Fathers benefit, too!

- Look at little things that give messages to men about their place in the program. *Stronger Together* (Lee, 2004) suggests, for example, to think about the following:
  - Is the initial interview, if there is one, scheduled so that both parents can attend?
  - Does the application form ask for the name, address, and phone number of the noncustodial parent or the mother's significant other?
  - Are men on the mailing list to receive all of the announcements, invitations, questionnaires, and bulletins?
  - Are parent-teacher conferences scheduled so that both parents can come, and are both parents expected to come?
  - Can men see and interact with other men in the classroom or at the center?
- Consider these ideas for getting men into the center if hiring male teachers is difficult:
  - Male bus drivers can double as classroom aides.
  - High school and college students could volunteer as part of a class assignment.
  - Community service clubs could send males to spend time with the children.
- Decide that men want to be involved, and then proceed to include them in the decisions about *how* they want to be involved. Don't expect them to be automatically interested in everything that women teachers and mothers find engaging.
- Increase father involvement in your program by using some of these ideas:
  - Create activities especially for men. For many years, Ethel Seiderman's husband Stanley held Saturday morning breakfasts for fathers at the child care center where Ethel was once director.
  - Hold an annual Father's Day picnic.
  - Have a father organize the other fathers for a workday in the center, classroom, or play yard. Mothers can be included, but if a father organizes it, men are more likely to come.
  - Research the best times to hold parent-teacher conferences so that fathers can come. Afternoons won't work for all fathers (or for all mothers).
  - Have family parties where everybody is invited, including fathers and even grandfathers.

25 TAKING A TRANSFORMATIVE APPROACH TO PARENT EDUCATION

WHAT TEACHERS NEED TO KNOW

Many people think of education involving a teacher and a learner who each have separate roles. The teacher teaches, and the learner learns. In early childhood programs, this idea can apply to children and also to parents when the program where their children go has a parent education component. In this particular model, the learner is the parent, and the teacher is the early childhood professional or some other expert. This view of education is based on the idea that the teacher has a body of knowledge and a set of skills; the goal, therefore, is to transmit the knowledge and skills to the learner.

A different model involves a two-way process in which the roles of teacher and learner are more fluid and dynamic. This model looks at the teacher and the learner sharing roles. In this model, teachers are most effective when they also see themselves as learners. They get to know their students, who they are, what they are interested in, what they know and can do, what they need to know and be able to do, and how best they can learn. Teachers also learn, mostly by observing, where the learning edge of each student lies. Lev Vygotsky, a Russian theorist, used the term *Zone of Proximal Development* (or *ZPD*) for the student's learning edge—that is, what each student is ready to learn next.

Parent education comes in many different forms. It becomes transformative when the teacher and learner share information in such a way that both learn something.

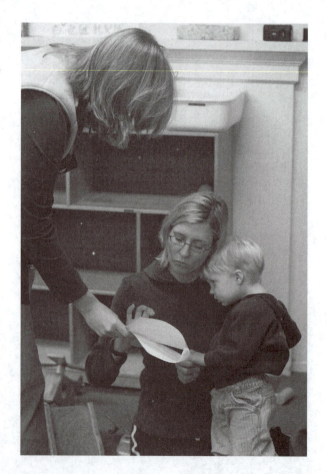

Using these ideas of teacher as learner and student as teacher, it is possible to move away from parent education that is based on a knowledge transmission model and move toward what is called a transformative education model. In simple terms, transformative education is when two people or groups come together and, through their interactions, are both changed for the better. Transformative education, as it relates to parent education, assumes that both teacher and family have bodies of knowledge that complement each other. Transformative education is vital when diversity is present. And diversity is always present, even among groups of people who look like they are from the same background, race, or culture. Dig a little deeper, and you will find generational, religious, economic, gender, age, and ability differences, just for starters.

Transformative education doesn't preclude holding workshops or creating classes in parenting or offering books and other resources for the parents' edification. It just means that the teacher realizes there are a variety of perspectives on everything relating to education and child care. He is sensitive to differences and seeks to understand them. It's a matter of openness rather than persuasive salesmanship. Teachers can gain a great deal of knowledge themselves through a transformative education process.

Looking at a situation where obvious diversity is present, imagine an immigrant family who is new to a school or other early care and education program. When the early childhood professional is using a transformative education model, she doesn't just set out to teach them child development or how to improve their child's academics. She also works to learn what she can about who they are and what they want for their child. She explains (through a translator, if necessary) how the program works, and she also asks about their expectations. She asks about schools and other early care and education programs in their country and how they are the same or different from here. Her motive is to discover where there's a fit, and what might cause them discomfort, in this program. She doesn't do this all at once, but slowly, over time, while working on the relationship. Both parties—the family and the teacher—gain from their many conversations and get to know each other as well. Trust builds.

It may seem like a luxury to have so many conversations with a family. See Strategy 31 for ideas on how to find and create opportunities to talk to families.

WHAT TEACHERS CAN DO

- Work on building a relationship with each family. Get to know them.
- Establish from the first day you meet the family and their child that you want to learn about them, including their dreams for their child and their ideas about how to fulfill them.
  - CAUTION: Be careful to go slowly. Mention your goal, but before going further, consider their response. Are they suspicious, insecure, or hesitant to reply? Some families have many experiences of being questioned by authorities who had control over their lives. You want to develop a different kind of relationship, so be careful not to ask too many questions or leave them feeling like they have been interrogated.
- Keep an open mind. If a family tells you they want something that you disagree with, suspend judgment until you are sure you understand them. In the face of cultural or economic differences, misunderstandings are easy.
- Don't just ask questions. Observe as well, and comment on what you see. Sometimes asking questions doesn't work as well as just remarking about what strikes you.
- Encourage the family to observe in the classroom or program if they have time and are comfortable doing so. Ask them to comment on what they see, and listen to them with an open mind.
- Become aware of your own stereotypes, and put them aside along with your judgments. Make your goal to get to know this family uncluttered by stereotypic images.
- Notice when something a family member says or does causes discomfort in you. Being aware of your own reactions gives you some clues about where you need to learn more.
- Besides your daily work and the interactions with each family, put together a more formal parent education program, which can include the following:
  - Special meetings with a topic that parents agree is one they want to know more about. Be sure to have translators for families who need them.
  - Discussion groups about issues that come up in which parents have an interest.
  - Home visits, if parents are comfortable with the idea.
  - Opportunities for observation and discussion with you.
  - A resource area with information that parents can use.

26 WORKING WITH PARENTS AROUND HOLIDAY ISSUES

WHAT TEACHERS NEED TO KNOW

Many early childhood teachers love holidays and spice up their curriculum with traditional seasonal celebrations. Some even create a holiday curriculum as a main course, not just a spice. As awareness of diversity began to grow, however, some teachers began to question their holiday curriculum, because it didn't include everyone. Some then decided to expand to include different cultures and religions. That change made November and December packed with holidays as teachers worked to squeeze in Columbus Day, Halloween, the Day of the Dead, Ramadan, Diwali, Thanksgiving, Hanukkah, Christmas, Kwanza, and Los Santos Reyes. Whew! They barely got to rest until it was Martin Luther King, Jr., Day, Chinese New Year, and then Valentine's Day.

One problem with a holiday curriculum is the mandate regarding separation of church and state. An issue with adding diversity to the holiday curriculum, even if you leave religion out, is that it is easy to pass on misinformation. Children may learn more about stereotypes than they do about true cultural differences. Another issue is that some holidays are bound to be neglected no matter how hard the teacher tries to include all cultures. It can get to be just too much! A fairly common response to the overwhelmingly diverse holiday curriculum is to eliminate *all* holidays, which some programs and schools now mandate.

On the positive side, holidays can be a way to involve parents and to further relationships between home and school. Wonderful things can happen when parents and other family members come into the classroom to share how they celebrate a particular holiday. When teachers take into consideration the age of the children in the group and who the children are, incorporating holidays into the curriculum can be done in ways that are developmentally appropriate, relate to the educational needs of the children, help them appreciate diversity, affirm their identity, and end up being relevant and meaningful.

WHAT TEACHERS CAN DO

- Take the age of the children into consideration. The younger the child, the less meaning holidays have, and the less they learn from them. School-age children can enjoy and appreciate some disruptions in their day and are more apt to learn something from those disruptions than younger children are. For example, infants and toddlers feel more secure and, therefore, in more of a learning mode when their daily schedule stays somewhat the same. Holiday celebrations can create big disruptions, especially when there is a big fuss over them.

- Be clear about your goals for including holidays in the curriculum. If one goal is to expand an antibias curriculum, learning about and/or experiencing a wide variety of holidays can affirm cultural identity in some children and help others appreciate traditions that are different from their own.

- If another goal is to include parents in meaningful ways, holidays may be able to promote that goal. On the other hand, diverse holiday celebrations may be a deterrent to building a relationship with some parents. Get to know the families of the children in your class or group, and discover how each feels about holidays before you move forward with a holiday curriculum. Be sensitive to and respectful of families who don't celebrate any holidays or families who worry about their children being exposed to holidays other than the ones their family celebrates.

Taking an antibias approach means recognizing the cultures in the class when celebrating holidays.

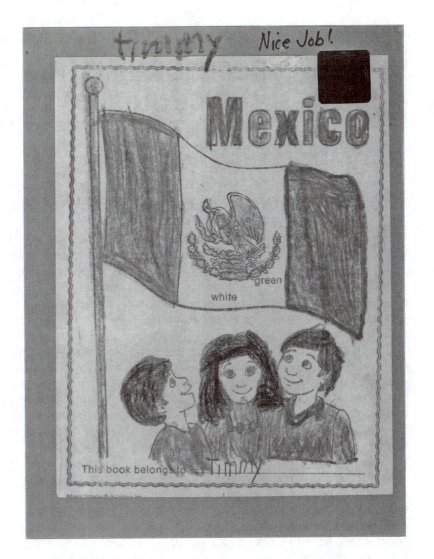

- If you plan to include holidays, decide whether to stick to the ones represented by the families in the class or group or to introduce unfamiliar ones. It may be you have plenty of diversity and you don't need to go outside it. Or you may want to bring in something new that the children aren't familiar with, especially if it is celebrated by families in the local community, even though none of the families in your class or program celebrates it.
- Connect all holiday activities and/or lessons to real people rather than making generalizations, which can lead to stereotypes. Make sure you have accurate information.

I remember a December math activity from the classroom of one of my sons. The children were learning about charting. That day, the teacher stood in front of the class with a piece of chart paper divided vertically down the center. Across the top was written *Christmas trees*. The teacher then asked, "Who has their Christmas tree up? Raise your hand." The first column was labeled *Has Christmas tree up.* Check marks were made in that column for each hand that was up. Then, the teacher asked, "Who doesn't have their Christmas tree up yet? Raise your hand." Corresponding check marks were made in the second column. When I heard about the activity, I couldn't help but wonder what the children whose families don't celebrate Christmas felt during that activity, and what did they do? Did they just keep their hands down? Did the teacher notice? Did she count to see if some hands were missing? Did some children just put their hands up anyway, even if neither question pertained to them? Obviously, the teacher made some assumptions about the religious backgrounds of the children in her class. Sometimes diversity doesn't show, but there is always diversity of some kind in any group of children and their families. Apparently, this teacher missed that concept.

27 EXPLORING PARENTS' ROLE ON DECISION-MAKING BOARDS AND COUNCILS

WHAT TEACHERS NEED TO KNOW

In some schools and programs, family members are on an advisory board or council, and in some, they are the policymakers. Many schools have a parent-advisory group that gives input to school policies. Head Start is an example of a model that involves parents at all levels, including giving them an advisory role and, to some extent, a decision-making role. In parent participation preschools, the parent board is the decision-making body. Of course, not all schools or programs give parents this kind of power. For many, the family council is purely advisory, and professionals make the final decisions.

Having families in these advisory and decision-making roles means that the program is more likely to be responsive to their children in the ways they wish. Community connections can be greater when parents are involved in giving advice and setting policy. The program is more likely to be a firmer part of the community in which the families live and to be responsive to their needs. Playing these roles helps parents and other family members see that they can influence what happens in their children's lives. The benefits go beyond their own children as they develop and hone leadership skills that serve their communities.

When families serve on boards and councils, they have a greater voice than when they come as individuals and ask that the program be sensitive to what they want for their children. The teachers and staff in a program are often from a different culture or socioeconomic level than the families they serve. These teachers and staff may not have much power themselves to apply what they know and believe using the principles and practices they've learned in their teacher preparation courses. The policies they have to follow and/or the principles and practices they've learned may set them apart from the families they serve, and communication may be blocked. (See Strategies 16, 17, and 18,) Parent voices are usually quiet when they come individually—and even the loud ones eventually move on to the next grade or program. Having parent boards and councils allows voices to be heard in a different way and provides continuity as well as flexible responsiveness as the board changes over time.

Parent boards and councils benefit teachers, principals, directors, staff, and caregivers as well, by broadening their views as they come to understand perspectives that may be different from their own. When the council or board is working well, professionals enjoy additional support that they might not otherwise experience.

Encouraging leadership among the families served will bring rich rewards. You have to get to know the families well enough to begin to discern leadership qualities. But what are those qualities? How do you know a leader when you see one? According to Debra Sullivan (2003), "Leaders are any individuals who influence others in a way that encourages them to higher or better performance and personal development. Effective leaders may or may not have authority, position, or status. They do, however, have integrity, dignity, and respect for others. Leaders empower, encourage, and support others in a shared effort to achieve goals or create change.... They take action where action is needed and they enable others to take action when another person's strengths and ability are needed" (p. 7).

This advisory group of parents and teachers meets regularly throughout the school year. This particular meeting focused on spending some money that was allocated for school improvement.

Sunny Valley School
May 13

Minutes of the Sunny Valley School Site Council meeting held on May 12.

In attendance: Sharon Allen, Latanya Miller, Sandy Smith, Dena Mundy, Sage Johnson, Dean Ames, and Juana Gomez.

The meeting was called to order at 3:39 by Chairperson Juana Gomez. Minutes of the April 14th meeting of the School Site Council were read and approved.

Latanya Miller presented the Council with two copies of the District Mater Plan for School Improvement which outlines the regulations regarding all aspects of school improvement. The district has asked the site council for input concerning possible changes in the Master Plan. Site Council members were asked to review the plan and make appropriate suggestions.

Ms. Miller indicated that the School Improvement Plan budget project for the next year is $14,501, approximately 4,000 less than this year's budget. She also noted that the future of the program is still uncertain.

After a review of the district philosophy relating to student behavior, the Council discussed and composed a discipline plan for use at Sunny Valley School. The plan outlines area of responsibility for students, parents, teachers and administrators.

Ms. Miller distributed copies of the School-wide Environment component composed by the Council at the April meeting.

The meeting was adjourned at 4:43.

Dean Ames,
Secretary

WHAT TEACHERS CAN DO

- Help each family understand how the program, organization, or school works so that they have a bigger picture than if they only tuned into their own and their child's experiences with the caregiver, staff, or teacher.
- Look at your own attitudes. (See Strategy 7, Removing Barriers to Partnerships.) Openness to parents' perspectives is essential for working with parent boards and councils.
- Learn to look for leadership qualities, even in shy, quiet people. Who has vision? Who wants to make something happen? Who has influence on others? Who can work both independently and interdependently? These qualities may not show up readily. You may have to look hard for them, but you will be richly rewarded as you become increasingly aware of people with leadership potential among the families.

Part of the process of creating a board or council is recruiting parents. Individual parent voices may be ignored but when parents come together on parent boards and councils their voices may command more attention.

- Mentor new leadership. Encourage and give support to these potential leaders. Provide training for them. Head Start is known for developing leaders—not only in the program, but also in the community. A common Head Start story is the bringing up of parents through the ranks of the profession, starting as a parent volunteer and eventually working as a staff member, a teacher, or even a director or other administrative position.

28 CREATING ENVIRONMENTS FOR COMMUNICATION

WHAT TEACHERS NEED TO KNOW

An environment influences behaviors as well as shapes thoughts and creates feelings in people—both adults and children. We behave one way in a library, another way in a bank, a different way in a workout room, and yet another way in a place of worship. The environment gives us messages about how to behave. Part of growing up is learning how to read those messages. Early childhood professionals are aware of this phenomenon and often take care to arrange their environments so that children get the right messages about how they should behave there. Take a library space in a classroom, where the goal is to settle down and enjoy books—the area is set up to be comfortable, cozy, relaxed, and relatively quiet. That library corner is a contrast to the play space in an infant center, where physical exploration is a goal and the room is set up to encourage children to move freely rather than snuggle in.

It may not be easy to set up environments that invite parents into the classroom or center, but when it is possible, it's a worthy goal. In any program, the entry space can give a welcoming message. If the space is limited, it might be a simple message, such as a bulletin board with pertinent items displayed. The most likely place to see more elaborate environmental arrangements made for parents is in a preschool or infant center, where family members deliver and pick up their children. Some programs have cubbies that family members can use for messages or notices. Of course, a couple of comfortable chairs, a table, a coat rack, and a steaming pot of coffee (out of reach of the children) are other welcoming devices. For parents who bring younger siblings with them to pick up their children, some readily available, simple toys or baby books say welcome to other family members, too. If parents spend time in the program itself, either as observers or as volunteer helpers, another welcoming sign is a place for parents to safely store their belongings. An example of a strong environmental invitation in an infant center would be a place for breast-feeding mothers to feel relaxed and comfortable. The message here is that they are welcome to come in to feed their babies.

Many things work against inviting parents through environmental means besides lack of space or funding for adult furniture. If children are bused, the families may not come on a daily basis but only for enrollment procedures, conferences, meetings, or open houses. The spaces for these events may be functional but usually are not very warm and welcoming. That's the common situation. This chapter hopes you'll think beyond *what is* in order to start conceiving of *what can be*. Until early childhood professionals raise their sights and envision better spaces than are the norm, there isn't much hope for change. Much of this book is based on visions and hopes for change.

WHAT TEACHERS CAN DO

- Analyze the environment you are in right now, and think about how it affects your behaviors, thoughts, and feelings.
- Analyze the early childhood environment you are most familiar with, and figure out what messages it may be giving parents. Try to imagine yourself as a parent bringing your child into the classroom. Think about what environmental arrangements could be made to make you feel welcome.
- Help parents get to know the teacher and staff of the classroom or center by putting up a bulletin board with pictures of anyone who works with their children. Include their names, what they

Although this is the area where the staff stores their children's books, it serves double duty as a space where adults can get away and talk in private. The adult-size furniture offers more comfort than small chairs, and the round table gives the two a chance to sit closer to each other.

want to be called, and a short biography. Getting to know who is in and around their child's classroom helps parents feel more secure and at home.

- If parents only come occasionally, be sure that when they do come, they feel welcome in the spaces they visit. Put some thought into those spaces.
- Consider the entryway. What is there that gives these messages: "Welcome. Come in. Make yourself at home."
- Consider the registration area and reception area. Do parents feel they belong here? What signs tell you that other family members are welcome? Are there toys for children while their parents sign up or sign in? Is the area wheelchair accessible? Is there evidence of what kind of program this is, such as child-centered decorations or products? Does the area take aesthetics into consideration?
- Consider the furniture arrangements. In the office, is the visitor's chair across from the desk where the principal or director sits? Though you may not be able to suggest it, even such a simple device as moving the chair out from behind the desk and next to the visitor's chair changes a formal atmosphere to a warmer, friendlier one.
- How much of the natural environment is visible? Is there natural lighting, with windows looking out at trees or plants? Is there an outdoor area for parents to make themselves comfortable?

29 EMPOWERING SELF AND OTHERS

WHAT TEACHERS NEED TO KNOW

What does empowerment mean? That depends on your definition of power. If you equate power with control and domination, then empowerment of parents and family members doesn't make sense. To consider a different definition, look to the origins of the word *power*, which comes from the Latin root meaning "to be able." Looking down that path brings one to the idea of what is sometimes called *personal power*. Personal power can be defined as the ability to be who you really are. Intisar Shareef, a community college professor, takes personal power a step further and consider it to be the ability to define your own reality and have others accept it. Her definition takes power beyond the personal and into the interpersonal—indeed, into the political realm. I see personal power as what is behind interpersonal and political power. All these aspects of power are important, and none need have anything to do with domination.

Watch the interactions between two people closely; sometimes their body language tells you that one is trying to dominate the other. Here is an example of such an interaction: A parent storms into the director's office after pushing aside a secretary who tries to stop him. He strides across the room and stands with his hands on the director's desk. He leans way over so that his face is close to hers and says, "My child is a vegetarian and your teachers are feeding her meat!" His expression bristles with rage as he waits for her response. Note how both his verbal and his nonverbal communication put him in the top-dog position—just like in a real-life dogfight, where one dog dominates the other. This human interaction is about winning and losing. The parent is out to win the fight, and depending on how the director responds, he just may intimidate her enough to consider himself the winner. This may be dog nature, but it isn't human nature—it is learned. And anything that is learned can be unlearned. Empowering parents and other family members is about helping them find and use their personal and interpersonal power and avoid using dominant and submissive behaviors.

Some people enjoy jockeying for power. Two people who are equally good at playing the dominating game may switch positions throughout an interaction, leaving no clear winner at the end. Even if one wins, the loser may enjoy the game enough to keep playing it the next time they interact. Other people don't jockey for position but immediately make themselves submissive when interacting with someone who is even a little dominating. Let's look at an example of how that works. The issue is the same, but this time, it is a different parent: A mother comes into the office after learning that her vegetarian child is being given meat in the child care center. She stops at the secretary's desk and asks to see the director. The secretary says that the director is on the phone and that she will have to wait in the hall outside the office, because there is no room for her inside. The mother retreats to the hall and finds the only chair is a child's chair. She sits down on it. After 15 minutes, she checks with the secretary, who apologizes for forgetting her and ushers her into the director's office. The director sits behind a rather large desk, where he is reading some papers, and doesn't look up when the mother enters. The mother stands silent, shifting her weight from foot to foot. The director finally looks up, paper still in hand, and murmurs "Yes?" before looking back down at the paper. The person with the power in this situation is the director. We don't know if the mother made herself submissive or was forced into the role by the secretary and director's actions. If being the underdog is her usual role, it's possible that she'll switch roles in interactions with people she perceives as weaker than herself—such as children.

WHAT TEACHERS CAN DO

- Recognize that the domination system is not natural but is learned. Furthermore, the system is supported by the institutions of the society. That means that not everyone is born with the same chance to win in the domination game. Groups targeted for bias on the basis of race, culture, gender, age, class, ability, or sexual orientation have a harder time dominating than do those who enjoy the privileges that the society automatically gives them. Not that all people in nontargeted groups play the domination game, but if they do, it is easier for them to win than it is for people in targeted groups, especially if those in the targeted groups have internalized their oppression. Of course, not all people in targeted groups submit to domination. Many are outstanding game players, but even if they are good enough to win, institutionalized bias makes sure that they never get in a position to play the dominating game with those who control the institutions. Until we all recognize how the domination system operates, and then work to dismantle it, we won't be fully effective at empowering children and their families.

- What professionals can do is help family members tap into their personal power—the form of power that everyone has. When personal power is acknowledged and nourished, people are able to show who they really are. They don't need to dominate others, and they can resist being put in a submissive position through internalized oppression (when the messages of the oppressor guide the person from the inside).

- Help family members "find their voice," which is the way people express their personal power.

- Empower yourself. Start by becoming aware of how you react to perceived threats by becoming defensive. If the director in the story above had responded to the dominating father by meeting him head-on or putting up a protective shield, the result would have been blocked communication. If instead she brought her personal power to the situation, she could have responded as her authentic self and given a nondefensive reaction, perhaps surprising the father out of his dominating stance.

30 COMMUNICATING THROUGH WRITING

WHAT TEACHERS NEED TO KNOW

Attempts should be made to communicate with family members in every medium possible. Writing is one major way to get messages across. Throughout the history of early childhood education, teachers and parents have communicated with each other through writing.

Although not yet universal, e-mail messages have become a major way of communicating with some parents. Notes, messages of concern, requests to make appointments, newsletters, articles, and most things that used to go home on paper can now be sent by e-mail. This is especially useful in corporate child care programs, where such communication can be timely and immediate and is especially useful if children and parent are located in the same building. Be considerate about flooding parents with too much—a problem with technology. In the past, the problem was not enough communication; now, it is so easy to send an e-mail with an attachment that it is sometimes overdone.

Attempts should be made to communicate with family members in every medium possible. Written notices are one important way to get messages across.

This letter goes home to families the first week of school. It is intended to give them a brief introduction to the classroom that will tide them over until Back-to-School Night.

First Grade
Ms. Ritz
Monte Vista School

First grade is an exciting year because children expand their learning incredibly, exert their competence and and develop independence. My goals for all children are to

- support learning by assessing the appropriate activities that will challenge children without discouraging them;
- encourage children to find their strengths so they can feel proud of their accomplishments;
- help children find strategies to become self-motivated learners.

This is a "Can Do" classroom. First graders can do lots of things!

<u>Behavior:</u>

Lifeskills teach children the language of responsible behavior. Our classroom will use <u>Lifeskills</u>, <u>I messages</u>, a <u>Peace Table</u> and <u>Classroom meetings</u> to make sure students have all the knowledge needed for successful behavior.

No one's perfect. On horrible, no good, very bad days, anyone might need some time out. In our class it is called Australia. Children who are sad, angry, etc. can spend a few minutes quietly there to regroup for learning.

For problems between peers the Peace Table is a place to give and receive I messages without disturbing others.

Repeated disruptive behavior that interferes with learning can occur. Children will bring home a **Lifeskill Homework note**. Please discuss the problem, suggest some strategies or solutions, sign and return.

I'm sure you'll have questions and concerns as time goes on. Please communicate any concerns as they arise. Ask questions, share ideas, offer help. These are ways to get in touch with me:

- You can send a note in your child's folder.
- Leave a post-it on the "moon table" during Family Reading.
- Phone the school: 792-4531.

    If it can't wait until the next day, call my home before 9 pm: 578-8052.

- Send me e-mail: kritz414@sbcglobal.net

Let's have a great year!

WHAT TEACHERS CAN DO

- Use e-mail for those parents who read and respond to e-mail. But don't use it exclusively. Be sure to use other means to reach parents who either don't have or don't use e-mail regularly.
- Use personal notes to communicate about a variety of things. It doesn't take long to jot down a little note on a piece of paper and send it home with the child. Subjects for notes can be positive comments about the child, something he or she did or said, and an appreciation of some contribution he or she made to another child or to the class. Of course, thank-you notes to family members for their contributions are not only a social nicety but also a way to let parents know they are appreciated.
- Happy-grams are easy-to-use, commercial notes to send home bits of good news about a child. Usually, they have smiley faces and a place to fill in blanks. You can also make them by hand— you don't need commercial ones. These can be a real bonus for parents who are used to notes coming home about misbehavior instead of good news.
- The opposite of happy-grams for some families may be assessment reports. For kindergarten and primary students, these may be in the form of report cards or test results. Certainly, it's better for any assessment results to be discussed with families in person rather than to be sent home on a piece of paper, but the reality is that such things do happen.
- Communicate with families through newsletters. Newsletters help parents know what is going on in the classroom. Having an idea of recent themes, activities, and events helps them talk to their

children about their experiences. Newsletters also clue family members in to upcoming events. They can serve as a means of connecting families to each other, especially when they contain news items pertaining to families. Other uses of newsletters can be to help parents understand the purposes of various activities and give ideas for carrying on at home themes and activities that originate in the classroom. The newsletters can also ask for ideas or recipes from families; thus, the newsletter becomes a two-way communication device.

- Communicating through the use of bulletin boards is another way of communicating through writing. Some parents who don't interact a good deal with the teacher or staff may use bulletin boards as important sources of information. Here are some ideas for effective bulletin boards:
  - Put bulletin boards in a location where they are clearly visible and accessible.
  - Label the bulletin board so that parents know it is for them. Make it attractive, and keep it up to date. If it always looks the same, parents will stop looking at it.
  - Items on the bulletin board should respond to the specific interests of the families enrolled.
  - The bulletin board can include such items as recipes for play dough, guidelines for choosing books or toys, announcements of coming events, and lists of community resources.
  - Pertinent articles of interest to parents are useful. If the article is short, it can just be posted. If the article is longer, copies should be available for family members to take home.
- Some programs have a daily bulletin—often handprinted on a white board—that gives parents who pick up their children the highlights of what went on that day. This bulletin is more timely than a newsletter and more visible than an item on the bulletin board. Such a device can provide parents with conversation starters when they talk to their children. The question "What did you do today?" sometimes is answered with "Nothing." It often works better to mention something specific, such as "How did you like making tortillas today?"
- Consider using two-way journals. This written device is especially effective in infant-toddler programs, where daily two-way communication is vital in order to meet the child's needs. A two-way journal is used during the day by the staff to record events and details of caregiving, from amounts eaten to diaper contents and changes. Of course, other items of interest can also be included. At the end of the day, the journal goes home with the family, who records what caregivers need to know the next day—how well the baby slept, when he or she ate, and any notable differences in routine. Mood changes can be indicators of the onset of illness and should be noted as well.
- Some programs have a parent library and make books and articles available to borrow.
- Some programs collect pamphlets from community resources and make copies available to parents.

A story: One kindergarten had a traveling teddy bear that was accompanied by a journal intended to record his adventures in the homes he visited. The bear and the journal came in a backpack and went home with a different child each weekend. The idea was for a family member to read parts of the journal to the child and help him or her write additional journal entries, which could be dictated by the child and written by the parent.

This communication is designed to involve parents at home in working on specific skills that the child needs at school.

To the folks at _____ house,
   Your child needs extra practice in
_____.
Please spend some time working with your child on this skill. A little attention now will make a big difference later on.
   Thanks,
      KITTY KITZ

31 HOLDING ONGOING CONVERSATIONS WITH FAMILIES

WHAT TEACHERS NEED TO KNOW

Finding time to talk with families is not an easy task for early childhood professionals. When children come on a bus, or walk to school on their own, teachers may not even see the parents. In prekindergarten programs, parents sometimes arrive with their children and come back to pick them up, which means the teacher sees them, but it's a busy time for everybody. Teachers and caregivers do see families face to face, but it's not the best time of the day if parents are in a hurry or come back tired. Even so, teachers and caregivers can't wait for the perfect opportunity.

Daily conversations can be an important way to get to know each other. In many programs, these conversations are the main form of parental involvement and serve an important function of making the parent a part of the program. It can be a time to exchange information on child- and family-related issues.

Not every school sees parents on a daily basis, but some have a policy that a family member take their child to the classroom to ensure daily contact between the teacher and the family member. When family members don't come to school or to the program, telephone conversations can supplement face-to-face contact. Use these conversations to ask about absenteeism or to share a personal observation or anecdote about a child. Although it may be difficult to accept calls from families during working hours, letting them know what times are best to call gives them the possibility of initiating a conversation. Some teachers make themselves available for telephone conversations on a regular basis and let families know when that is. Nap time is a favorite among child care providers and all-day preschool teachers.

WHAT TEACHERS CAN DO

- Greet parents by name every time you see them, and make a point to say good-bye. If you can squeeze in a conversation after the greeting or before the good-bye, parents will feel more valued. That's the way to grow a relationship.
- Make positive remarks about their child whenever you talk to the parents.
- If the child is present, include him or her in the conversation. It's disrespectful to talk around children as if they don't exist.
- The attitude of the professional gives messages about whether it's okay to have a conversation or if this is just a quick encounter. Try to unbusy yourself when family members arrive. It isn't easy when you have a group of children you are responsible for, but it is worth doing.
- If you have problems making yourself available for more than a hello and good-bye, try to figure out a way to do so. Make yourself available, even if it isn't easy. Some ways to do this are the following:
  ○ Suggest that parents visit or observe, and then make time to talk to them.
  ○ Stagger arrival and departure, if possible, so that everybody doesn't arrive at once.
  ○ Have an extra staff person come in during the times that parents are there.
- Although some teachers separate their private lives from their professional lives, others who live in the same neighborhood take time to talk when they run into family members of the children in their center, family child care home, or school.

Keeping in touch with families through regular conversations with them is important. It isn't always easy to find time, but this director is making time for a quick chat with a mother.

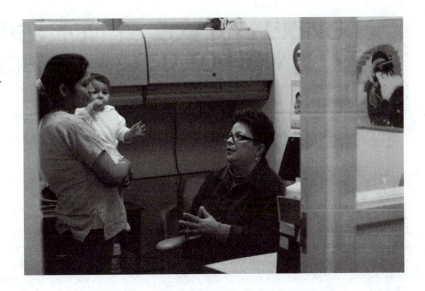

- Consider home visits if the program permits and parents are comfortable with them.
- Schedule conferences and meetings with families, either individually or with groups.
- Keeping records of contacts with parents help professionals discover if they are neglecting some families.

A story: A lonely grandfather who came to pick up his granddaughter stayed and stayed. The family child care provider had to move him toward the door so that she could get on with her work. One day, he remarked about the piano in the provider's family room. She asked if he played, and he replied that he did. She invited him to play something for the children. After that, he came on a regular basis and stayed for a half hour playing for the children. Eventually, he started giving lessons to some of the children. Everybody was happy about the arrangement!

32 LOOKING AT NONVERBAL COMMUNICATION ACROSS CULTURES

WHAT TEACHERS NEED TO KNOW

Nonverbal behavior is like a secret code that is understood but not talked about. Meaning never comes in words alone, but also relates to posture, movement, facial expressions, eye movements, gestures, and how close or how far away we stand. We must be able to pick up silent messages sent with or without words. We all read these messages effectively everyday, except when we meet someone who has a different system of nonverbal communication. That's when miscommunication occurs.

For example, miscommunication may occur when someone from Mexico watches an Anglo explaining a child's height by holding a hand out with the palm down. Although this gesture is easily understood by many people in the United States, a person from Mexico might find it very strange, because that particular gesture is only used for measuring objects. To measure people, the index finger is pointed up at the appropriate height. This may not be a big issue, and it perhaps will be laughed off by the Mexican person. Nevertheless, the message received is different from what was intended.

A bigger issue occurs when a teacher touches a child on the head and the parent worries that the gesture has stolen the child's spirit. Some people from Southeast Asia attach deep significance to a hand on the head. To other people, touching someone on the head is a sign of affection and a way they express love or comfort to dogs or children. Most of those people would never touch adults above the shoulders, however, and would not touch the president of the United States at all except to shake his hand if it were offered. Rules about touching are governed by status and power issues and are tied into respect. How, when, where, and why we touch each other is cultural. No one explains the rules, but we learn them. Cultural learning is subtle and starts very early.

Touching patterns vary greatly from culture to culture. Touch is just one example of a cultural difference that affects communication. Personal space is another. How close we stand or sit to or whether we breathe on people we are talking to holds cultural meanings. A person who comes from a "close culture" feels she is being shunned when someone from a more distant culture backs off. The person backing off may feel crowded and find the experience awkward or offensive, and she may even feel afraid. If she feels angry, she may be tempted to say, "Get out of my face!" Yet the person who comes too close in the name of friendliness may feel that the person who is backing off is either weird or a cold, uncaring person. Each reads the message from the other in a way that is different from what was intended.

Eye contact is another example of cultural difference. Learning about eye contact patterns starts in infancy. For example, in cultures where babies are constantly carried on their mothers' backs, intimacy is not necessarily expressed by eye-to-eye gaze. One common pattern of eye contact in the United States is for the listener to look directly at the speaker and for the speaker to gaze into the listener's eyes but also look away occasionally. Someone with this pattern who talks to someone with a different eye contact pattern may feel uncomfortable. He may even regard the listener who doesn't look at him as shifty, dishonest, or disrespectful. "Look at me when I talk to you" is sometimes heard from teachers whose students' eye contact patterns don't necessarily match their own. The listener who is expressing respect by keeping his eyes lowered or looking elsewhere when being spoken to may be mystified by the speaker's reaction to this eye contact pattern.

"Don't stare!" is a cultural command to children, but this is not a universal no-no. In some cultures, it's not only polite to stare but expected. A member of a staring culture feels rejected when no one stares at him. In other cultures, staring is not only impolite but can be considered downright dangerous.

These two seem to be doing just fine reading each other's nonverbal communication, but they could have a problem if one moves in closer or the other steps back. The amount of personal space an individual feels comfortable with is just one aspect of nonverbal communication.

WHAT TEACHERS CAN DO

- Become consciously aware of nonverbal behaviors. Although you may be used to reading messages that come from posture, movement, facial expressions, eye movements, gestures, and relative distance, realize that across cultures, these behaviors don't necessarily mean the same thing. Look for communication problems below the level of words and their meanings. The goal is to expand your ability to pick up silent messages in the ways they are intended.
- Recognize your own patterns of nonverbal behavior. Most of us are unconscious of these until we meet someone who doesn't fit our patterns. Consider that even though your own may feel right, normal, or good doesn't mean that they are in any way to superior to another person's nonverbal behavior patterns.
- Recognize that learning unwritten cultural rules of nonverbal communication takes time and patience. The best approach is to be aware of differences and to read the feedback from the parent or family member exhibiting them. Try different approaches if you are picking up discomfort in your attempts to communicate.
- Sometimes you can talk about subtle behavior differences, but it takes sensitivity to bring them out without causing further discomfort and, perhaps, defensiveness. Having a relationship with the parent or family member you are talking to can help bring the issues to the surface and make those issue easier to discuss.
- Don't expect that just because you know a person's culture you can predict his or her behavior. Few cultural patterns are rigid or apply to all members of a culture. Furthermore, cultural patterns change when they come in contact with new patterns.

33 MEETING WITH FAMILIES FOR THE FIRST TIME

WHAT TEACHERS NEED TO KNOW

Laying the foundation for a relationship starts when parents first meet the teacher, provider, director, or caregiver. The meeting is different depending on whether the family is going to their local neighborhood public school or is choosing the program or family child care home from a number of available ones. Sometimes there is no choice, and the family is just glad to be accepted in the only program for which they qualify.

The first meeting may be set up for one family or may be a group meeting with all the families who are enrolling their children. There are likely to be forms to fill out. If the family has the forms ahead of time, they can bring them to the meeting and discuss them there. This may be a time that the early childhood education professional gets to know something of the child's history in the family. It's important that the professional explains how any information the parents give will be used.

In some programs, the first meeting with the family may be in their own home. Home visits, not just at the beginning but throughout the year, have long been a valuable part of early childhood education

Here is a fairly simple and straightforward form that supplies basic information about the family and the child and invites family members to volunteer in the classroom. It also gives the option of doing work at home for the class. Notice that the form asks for "parent(s) name(s)," which makes it appropriate for single-parent families and also for families with parents of the same sex.

Home/School Connection

Child's Name _____ Birthday _____

Parent(s) Name(s) _____

Siblings (names and ages) _____

_____

Address _____

Home Phone # _____ Work Phone # _____

Pets (kind/name) _____

Hobbies/Interests _____

_____

Name you want your child to learn to write:

First: _____ Last: _____

Some things you may want to know about my child: (use back if necessary)

_____

_____

_____

Are you interested in volunteering in the classroom? _____
Times of Availability: M_____ T_____ W_____ T_____ F_____

Are you interested in doing work at home? _____

Programs for children age 5 and under sometimes have a parent handbook that contains information the parents need. The table of contents for this parent handbook, from a developmental children's center, shows that it is full of specifics that many families will appreciate having in writing.

programs, though mostly in Head Start and some other preschools. There are many obstacles to teachers making home visits, but also many advantages if these obstacles can be overcome. Some advantages are seeing a child in the context of home and family and gaining a better understanding of who that child is. Home visits can give information about the child's interests, skills, and learning styles. Meeting the family on their own territory can solidify the relationship with the teacher and help that teacher see how the family members and child interact at home. In addition, the teacher can meet family members who never come to the school or center and learn about the resources they have to offer the program.

The first encounter with the parents sometimes involves dealing with a good deal of paperwork, including forms related to the family income level and other forms to be signed, acknowledging that the staff is required to report any suspected child abuse. That makes an unfortunate beginning if the emphasis is to be on human relationships.

When parents and professionals can just talk together and share information, they are off to a better start. Of course, it is useful to have parents fill out a form that lets them explain their child's particular needs, ways of expressing herself, and other important information. Parents also usually are grateful for written information about the program, although they may prefer to take it home to read it. If the meeting is designed to be comfortable, relaxing, and not overwhelming, it's a better start. Additionally, when a separate meeting is set up for each family, it creates a good chance to begin a relationship.

WHAT TEACHERS CAN DO

- Find out right away what the family members want to be called and what they want you to call their child. Tell them what you want to be called. Be aware of cultural differences in the use of names and titles. Some families may feel uncomfortable calling you by your first name, and even more uncomfortable letting their child call you that. Some families may want their child to call you "teacher" without using your name, which to you may feel uncomfortable but for them is an appropriate sign of respect for your position.
- Discuss possible separation issues the child might have when starting the program. Share ideas with the parents, and listen to theirs about how to help their child cope with feelings about separation.
- For the youngest children, having the first meeting in their own home allows them to meet the new adult in their life on their own home turf. In most cases, that is difficult, but when it works out, there are a number of benefits for both the child and the family.

Although it is important to prepare parents for the separation difficulties their children might have when they first start in a program, this family obviously didn't need much preparation. This child is happy to say good-bye!

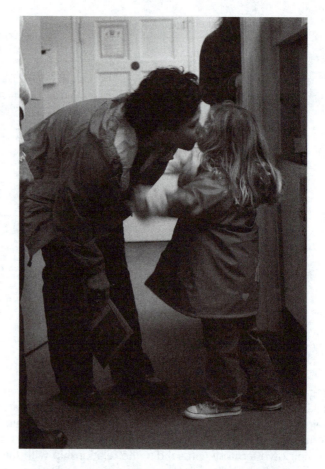

- If possible, invite the child and a family member to visit the program before the child actually starts in it. This pre-entry visit can ease the parents' minds as they watch the teacher interact with the child and see how things work in the program.
- If all the children are starting the program at the same time, staggering their entry can help them get more adult attention than if the whole group arrives the first day at the same time.
- Ideally, the first days should be short ones. That is not always possible, but it is worth aiming for.
- Although some programs have a policy about parents not staying in the classroom while their children are first adjusting, there are advantages to having a different policy. When parents ease their children into a program and are there for them at first, it not only sets a tone of welcome for the parents and their involvement but also makes the transition easier for the child. (See Strategy 38 on transition into a program.)
- Recognize that it's quite natural for some parents to have strong feelings about being separated from their children. Empathize with those parents, and avoid judging them as being too attached or overprotective. Parental emotions can be complicated and intense. They may experience feelings of ambivalence about leaving their children, worries about safety and quality of care, and fears about their child becoming attached to someone else. (See Strategy 8 on competition.)
- For those parents who have never separated from their child until this point, it may be helpful for them to know about the kinds of behaviors that are common in children. When this subject is discussed openly, it can relieve parents' minds that the early childhood professional isn't judging them or their child. Separation behaviors in young children can include:
  - Crying, clinging, protesting
  - Increased dependence
  - Difficulty in eating
  - Fears about going to sleep
  - Regressive behaviors—going back to an earlier stage in their lives—such as wetting their pants, thumb sucking
  - Passive behavior—as if they aren't quite "there".

34 THINKING ABOUT MEETINGS IN GENERAL

WHAT TEACHERS NEED TO KNOW

All types of meetings for parents can occur in early care and education programs. Several specific types are discussed in Strategies 35, 36, and 37 on conferences. Also the first meeting with families gets special consideration in Strategy 33. That's another specific kind of meeting. This chapter is about meetings in general, which can include parent discussion groups, informal support groups, planning meetings for fund-raising, planning meetings for field trips, board or counsel meetings, reading and study groups, and any other kind of meeting you can think of. Sometimes parents get together regularly to do crafts and talk.

Meetings are more effective if they are planned around what the families think they need rather than around what teachers think the families need. When parents and other family members have a chance to express what they want and share their interests, they may be more inclined to attend meetings. It's best if families choose and guide the agenda of meetings.

If some of the meetings are designed as "parent education," be sure that the format is an interactive one rather than the delivery of information from some expert. Although lectures may be interesting to some parents, this format fails to acknowledge that those in the audience have expertise as well. Delivering information in ways that ignore the competencies of the parents leads the relationship between staff and families away from partnerships. Strategy 25 discusses parent education further.

WHAT TEACHERS CAN DO

- Plan the size and style of the meeting so that it meets the parents' needs for comfort and provides an opportunity to talk with each other. Small groups create feelings of closeness, community, and ownership of the meeting. Meetings of one classroom or center are more effective than meetings of a whole school.
- Select a good time for the meeting. Get family input about the best date and time. Some parents find it enticing to come after work and have supper provided, followed by the meeting. Other parents who work close by can do "brown-bag" meetings at lunchtime.
- Provide child care, if needed.
- Be clear about the purpose of the meeting.
- Consider involving the children in making invitations to or refreshments for the meeting. Children can also provide decorations.
- Try to create a warm, friendly atmosphere where people feel like sharing.
- Use name tags if the parents don't know each other.
- Use icebreakers to help get participants acquainted with each other. Some kind of active exercise can help participants feel comfortable and relaxed. It creates a conducive atmosphere for interaction and sets a tone for the meeting.
- Plan meetings to encourage interaction among the participants. Discussions work better than lectures.
- Bring in interpreters, if needed, so that everyone understands everything.

Date _____

Dear _____,

    I really want you to come
to see _____
_____
in Room 28. Please come
Tuesday, _____
from 7:45 to 8:15 a.m.

    Love,

    _____

Estimada/o _____

Deseo que Ud. venga al "Open House" en el aula No. 28.

La clase estará abierta de las _____ a las _____.

Me gustaría mostrarle _____

Pienso que le gustaría ver _____

Una cosa que le quisiera leer es _____

_____

Two versions of an open house invitation—one in English and one in Spanish.

- Consider your role in the meeting. If you can be a facilitator rather than the person in charge, it's more likely that participants will interact with each other. As a facilitator, your role can be to provide some structure and ensure that everybody gets to talk.
- Don't think you have to be the only one planning and facilitating meetings. Let the families create a committee that takes over that job, or share the responsibility with them. Icebreakers for parent meetings include:
  - Play the "name game." Use a light-weight ball or a soft, throwable object for this icebreaker. Say the name of a participant, and then toss him or her the ball. Tell that participant to do the same until all the participants have been named aloud.
  - Pair up participants with people they don't know, and give them a few minutes to get acquainted with their partner. Have them introduce each other to the group.

35 HOLDING CONFERENCES

WHAT TEACHERS NEED TO KNOW

Conferences are designed to be a structured situation for the exchange of information and plans. They are more formal than the kinds of conversations that occur on a frequent basis between professionals and family members. This should be a time during which information is exchanged freely and questions and ideas are explored. One goal of a conference should be to further develop relationships, because this is a time when relationships can grow if handled carefully.

Conferences should not just be held to discuss bad news and unacceptable behavior, even though the term *progress report* has just those connotations in some primary programs. Families will start dreading conferences if they don't have any positive experiences with them.

There are many compelling reasons to hold conferences on an ongoing basis instead of just having casual conversations with families. Casual conversations often have audiences, and they can get interrupted. Just talking regularly may keep both sides informed about aspects of learning and development on a daily or weekly basis but may not give the overall picture. A conference is the time to focus and concentrate in a private, comfortable setting. If enough time is allowed, questions and concerns can be discussed, and misunderstandings can be cleared up. Conferences are good for providing the details as well as the bigger picture of learning and development, and they have the potential to increase knowledge when mutual sharing occurs. Conferences can be the time to discuss goals and plans as well as work to make sure that those of the program are compatible with those of the family.

WHAT TEACHERS CAN DO

- Recognize parents' feelings and expectations around conferences. Their own childhood experiences with schools, teachers, and grades can bring up unpleasant memories around parent-teacher conferences. Conferences can also bring up their hopes as well as their fears.
- Prepare for the conferences by making their purpose clear. If the purpose of the conference is to share information about a child's learning and development, plan ahead about how to do this sharing. Have specific examples of changes in the child since the last conference. Show examples from the child's work and play (including photos or video clips when possible) as well as stories and anecdotes. Be sure you include social and emotional progress as well as physical and cognitive progress. Collect records of actual incidents that show social-emotional growth. Use storytelling to show progress.
- Conferences should be explained when the family first arrives in the program. If there is a parent handbook, it should include written material about conferences so that parents don't think something is wrong when they are asked to attend a conference.
- Schedule conferences so that all families can come. Timing is important. If conferences are only held during the day, some family members may be excluded. If conferences are only held at night, others may be excluded. Ideally, conference scheduling should be flexible enough so that nobody is excluded.
- Open up conferences to any family member who wants to come, and watch out for thinking only of mothers when planning conferences. Fathers may be the most interested party, and sometimes grandparents may be as concerned with what happens at the program or school as the parents.

- Suggest the possibility of observation before the conference. Watching their child in action can help family members see what goes on in the program and how their child relates. It can also give them ideas about what to ask or comment on when they get to the conference.
- Think about ways to make family members feel at ease during the conference. Consider the setting and environment. (See Strategy 28, Environments for Communication, and Strategy 29, Empowering Self and Others.) Providing food or drink can help.
- Avoid using jargon. Explain in plain language what you want the parents to understand. Jargon puts you above the family and makes you an expert. You may be an expert, but so are the parents. Don't let expertise get in the way of communication or the relationship you should be building with each family.
- Don't compare a child to other children or to charts. Be careful of saying words like *fast*, *slow*, *behind*, or *ahead*. Growing up is not a race. Be aware of which words trigger feelings. *Normal* is a trigger word, and *abnormal* is even more of one. *Typically developing* or *atypically developing* are better terms. Talk about *challenges* rather than *problems*. Avoid labels or judgmental words; instead, use objective ways of talking about children—describe behaviors rather than labeling them.
- Check your attitude. (See Strategy 7, Removing Barriers to Partnerships.) Make sure that you and the parent are on the same side, figuratively and literally.
- Make sure that the conversation is two-way, not just a monologue on the part of the professional.
- Know your limits. Don't assume that you can be everything to every family. Don't expect that you have the solution to every situation. Don't stretch your knowledge and experience beyond their boundaries. Sometimes you need to bring in or refer parents to other resources. (See Strategy 46, Finding Community Resources and Making Referrals.)
- Respect confidentiality. Gossip is unprofessional, even when it is not harmful. Don't talk about one family to another.

Forms such as these may be used for the beginning-of-the-year conferences. Parents have the opportunity to express the dreams, wishes, and needs of their children at conferences held during the first month of school. Responsibility is shared by parent, student, and teacher.

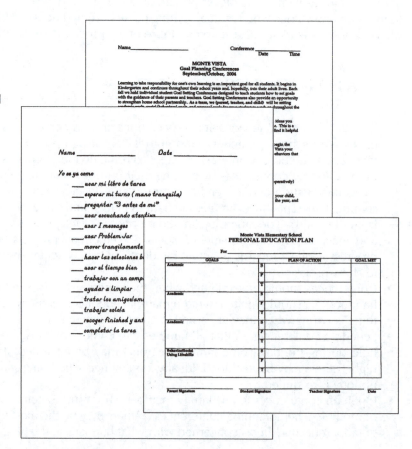

Conferences are designed to be a structured place to exchange information and make plans. They are more formal than the kinds of conversations that occur on a frequent basis between professionals and family members.

- Help parents to problem solve, but don't expect problems to be solved quickly or neatly. Your role is to help parents sort things out if they ask you for solutions or advice. You can share your knowledge and experience, but they need to come to their own conclusions.

A story: Four-year-old Kai was playing by himself on the floor with blocks and small figures. His voice could be heard across the room, talking nonstop. He manipulated the figures, creating dramatic action while they talked loudly to each other. Kai placed two figures on top of a block tower, and one was hanging down on a rope. The two on top kept looking at the dangling one, and they were having a loud argument when the teacher announced that it was snack time. Kai didn't stop playing. A few minutes later, the teacher approached him and insisted that he come to the snack table. "Awww," he protested. "Do I have to put things away?" he asked. "No, you can put a 'save sign' on what you have there" was the teacher's response. "Yeah," he said, "But I'll forget where I am." He looked forlornly at the two figures on top and the dangling one. "I'm sorry," said the teacher, "but you have to come now." Kai's face showed his distress, and he hung his head while folding his arms defiantly. Suddenly he looked up at the teacher and smiled. "I know what," he said confidently. "I'll just start a new episode." When the teacher told Kai's parents about this situation during a conference, they could see how their son was maturing. They were surprised that he used a word like *episode*, especially since they had no TV at home. They knew he had a great imagination, that wasn't a surprise, but this was the first time Kai's teacher had paid close attention to just how well he could play alone. The best thing about this story for both parents and the teacher was that it showed how Kai was making progress in coping with transitions.

36 CONSIDERING CROSS-CULTURAL CONFERENCES

WHAT TEACHERS NEED TO KNOW

The information in Strategy 35 on conferences also applies in cross-cultural situations. In addition, other barriers to communication may need to be addressed. The first one may concern concepts of time and what it means to be late. For some people, being early is important, so that when the appointed time comes, they are already there and waiting. For others, the goal is to walk in the door one minute before the scheduled time. They don't like to wait. For still others, forgivably late means 5 or so minutes, and some people don't consider 20 minutes after the scheduled time as truly late. Then for some people, clock time has very little meaning, and appointments may have even less. In their culture, arriving several hours or even days after the appointed time is within the bounds of courtesy.

Greetings have cultural rituals associated with them. Do you shake hands or not? What does a firm handshake mean? Does it mean you are a straightforward, competent person, or does it mean you are aggressive or rude? It depends on your culture. What does a slight touch mean in a handshake? Are you a weak person with limp hands, or are you shaking hands in the polite manner of your culture? What about eye contact? Are you respectful if you look someone in the eye, or are you disrespectful? It depends on your culture. And along with culture are gender issues. What is okay for men to do may not be okay for women.

If you want to be warm and friendly, do you smile and insist on being called by your first name? Do you call others by their first name? How you are received depends on the cultural meaning others give to your warm, friendly gestures. Instead of seeing you as open and welcoming, they may feel uncomfortable or think you disrespectful.

Do you like to get right down to business once the conference begins? For some people, it's important to socialize before getting to the point of the conference. Personal information about the family and each member may signal good manners for one family but feel uncomfortably intimate for another.

Of course, a huge barrier arises when families and professionals don't speak the same language. Strategy 35 on conferences addresses this issue when it relates to professional jargon, but that is a minor barrier compared to the one presenting itself when there is no common language between the program and the home.

One solution to these barriers is to become an anthropologist; however, even anthropologists don't understand all the cultural differences that may emerge in one school, classroom, or family child care center.

WHAT TEACHERS CAN DO

• See yourself as a lifelong learner. Studying differences may help, but the best approach is to tune up your sensitivity. There is always more happening than appears on the surface of any interaction, even between two people of the same culture and language group. The meanings of behaviors are what is important—and what you need to find out in order to be a good cross-cultural communicator. Observe, ask, read, listen, and discuss to find out which behaviors mean what to which people. The meanings may be cultural, but they may also be individual.

- Be prepared to make mistakes. You will make lots of mistakes. That's the way we learn. Regard each one as a learning situation rather than as a failure on your part.

- Assume responsibility for understanding all parents by finding translators, if needed, rather than expecting parents to bring their own translators. Be sure the translators are good ones. Also, make sure to provide all written notices in the languages of the families in your program.

- If family members speak your language somewhat but are embarrassed about their skills, help them understand that you are in the same or even worse situation regarding their language. It's important not to assume an attitude of superiority.

- When necessary, give up your agenda, and really listen to the parent—not only the words but also the feelings behind them. Listen until the person stops talking. Don't interrupt. When it's your turn, instead of arguing, educating, or responding from your own perspective, try to state the perspective of the other person. Put the gist or spirit of what you heard into words by making a statement about the other person's feelings, experience, perceptions, beliefs, or concepts. See if you can get at the deeper message. Most people do little of this kind of listening and responding. In a conversation where there is disagreement, most people constantly push forward their own point of view. Listening skills can be learned. Best of all is the feedback you get when you've received the message that someone was trying to send, because the communication opens up and the conversation continues.

- Connect parents from the same language backgrounds so that they can help and support each other. Also, introduce them to family members from other language backgrounds. Don't let language differences keep you from inviting all parents to participate in the program at whatever level they feel comfortable.

The following is a story about differences in concepts of time: A visiting professor arrived to teach a class in a country where time had a very different meaning. The first day, he arrived in class a few minutes early, and only one student was there. By the time the class was supposed to start, he had only a handful of students. "They'll be here," one of the early birds assured him. The class drifted in for the first hour, and eventually, the room filled up. The professor worried that he didn't have the full time period he had prepared for. When it was 5 minutes before the end of the class, the professor expected the students to start closing their notebooks and picking up their backpacks. Five minutes later, however, when the clocked clicked onto the closing time, not a single student had made a move to get ready to go. The class continued on for quite some time after the scheduled stopping time. The professor had a whole different sense of time to get used to.

37 TALKING WITH FAMILIES WHEN CONCERNS ARISE

WHAT TEACHERS NEED TO KNOW

Teachers and caregivers are often the first to notice that a child moves, behaves, interacts, learns, or communicates differently from other children. When you observe that you are not able to meet the child's needs, support his or her development, or foster his or her sense of belonging in the program, you may decide that the child needs more expertise than you have. That's an indication this is the time to have a meeting with the parents.

If you have a relationship with the parents and have been talking to them all along, the meeting about your concerns may not come as a surprise. It's quite possible that the parents, too, have been concerned and are glad to share their observations when they hear yours. Come to the meeting with notes on what you have observed and what kinds of interventions you may have tried. Some suggestions for conducting the meeting are listed below.

WHAT TEACHERS CAN DO

- Before putting together a meeting with the family in which you plan to discuss the possibility of getting outside help, do a series of observations. Note specifies. Objectively and in detail, describe the behaviors that give you cause for concern. Note when and where those behaviors occurred and under what circumstances. In conjunction with your observations, see if changing the environment or your approach affects the behavior. This is important information to share with the parents. Remember, it is only appropriate for you to discuss what you have observed about specific behaviors. Avoid the urge to label or diagnose.
- In the meeting itself, try to make the parents feel as comfortable and at ease as you can. Choose a seating arrangement that brings you together instead of separating you. Sitting behind a desk, for example, can make a psychological as well as a physical barrier between you and the parents. A warmer, friendlier arrangement may work better. Provide for privacy. Set aside enough time so that the meeting isn't rushed and you can talk things through. If this is the first such meeting the parents have had, they will need to feel that you care and that they can trust you.
- Start by asking the family how they see their child, and share any positive qualities you have observed. At the outset, let the family know that you are sharing your concerns to support their child's development and to get some ideas for how to best meet their child's needs. If the family differs in their view of the child, be open to their perspective, ask questions, gather information, and invite them to be your partner in meeting the needs of their child.
- Before you share your concerns with them, ask if they have any that they haven't already indicated. When it is time to share your concerns, be sure you communicate what you want to say clearly, without judgment, and with concrete examples. For example, rather than saying that a child is "behaving badly and bothering other children," give specifics—let the parents know that you have observed and documented that their child has a hard time sitting still and that he got up eight times while you were reading a story. Explain the behaviors that show you their child doesn't cope well with transitions. Tell about the five incidents of hitting other children during the last week. DO NOT suggest that a child has a specific diagnosis, such as attention deficit disorder.

- If the parents don't understand your concerns or disagree with you, they may be upset if you suggest that a referral for further assessment is necessary. It's possible that your observations will shock or anger them. In this case, sensitively supporting the parents' feelings is called for. Just as you accept the feelings of and empathize with the child, realize that the child's parents need the same approach. You're not a therapist, but some of the listening skills of a therapist can serve you well. Understanding that anger or blame are common responses for people in pain helps you accept the feelings without getting defensive. The point is to focus on the feelings of the parents and listen to what they have to say without minimizing their upset or trying to talk them out of it.

- Keep clear that further assessment is a positive move and that both you and the parents have the child's best interests at heart—even if you don't see eye-to-eye at the moment.

- Sometimes the family may not choose to access resources when you first share your concerns, or they may be open to information yet not take action immediately. Rather than label them as being "in denial" or something else, remember that everyone moves at a different pace and accepts information differently. The family's emotional response will affect what they are able to hear and understand. Processing and integrating this information will take varying amounts of time.

- Allow families time to accept that their child may be different than other children. That possibility is very hard for some families to hear. Unless there is a reason for urgency, let the family proceed at their own pace.

- Be prepared to support them in understanding what you have shared, repeating the information whenever necessary. Let them know that resource information is available whenever they want it. If you find that your own judgment or emotions about this interfere with your ability to respect the family as the decisionmaker, seek support for yourself, and don't be afraid to suggest that the family discuss this with someone else as well.

- Support the family in getting help. Let them know that you are there for them and for their child. If it comes to contacting an early intervention program, the school district's resources, or pediatrician/health care provider, let the family take the lead.

- Since many families will want to take action, be prepared to talk with them about resources for obtaining further assessment and/or possible services. This is the point at which you are "making a referral." It is generally appropriate to refer the family to their pediatrician at the same time you refer them to the local early intervention/special education resources. You should have information about services within your program, local early intervention services, special education services, and other resources.

- You cannot guarantee eligibility or services from another agency to a family. You can describe what might happen after the referral and what the possible outcomes might be based on what you've learned. You can also let the family know that you can be a source of information to the referral source. Parents must give permission for you to talk about their child with referral sources, so you will want to carefully respect the family's confidentiality and be sure that you have clear consent.

- When accessing resources, the family may face some barriers, including issues of insurance, language, cultural practices, and transportation. It's okay for you to set the process in motion for them, but rather than feeling responsible for overcoming all the barriers, focus on supporting the family and have faith that by letting them find their own ways to meet their child's needs, you serve the family and their child best (Brault, 2007).

38 HELPING THE CHILD ENTER THE SCHOOL OR PROGRAM

WHAT TEACHERS NEED TO KNOW

Preparations for the first day can start ahead of time when parents know that the child will be starting school or entering an early care and education program for the first time. It's good when parents can help their child get used to separation or a new situation in small doses. Often the children who have the most trouble separating upon entering a kindergarten, a new school, or other early childhood program are those who are away from family for the first time, although that is not always true. Ideally, the child also has some familiarity with the teacher or caregiver before the first day. (See Strategy 33, Meeting with Families for the First Time.) Those programs that are fully dedicated to partnering with parents sometimes figure out how to make home visits to the family before they start the program. This not only serves to meet the family on its home territory but also the child who is being enrolled. Another option is to invite the child and family to visit ahead of time so that the child can meet the teacher or caregiver and become familiar with the setting. Either of those approaches ensures that the child doesn't begin the first day in a strange place with a strange adult.

Some programs invite the parents to help their child enter the program for the first time by encouraging them to stay until the child is comfortable. This kind of invitation sets a warm tone and gives messages to both the child and family member that this is their place and they are welcome. This first experience can encourage parents to get involved in the program. Although some early childhood professionals would prefer that parents drop off their children and leave right away, there are some advantages in letting those parents who can and want to stay to do so.

A common situation is for a parent to want to sneak out without saying good-bye, because she knows her child will cling and cry. It is best to discuss the possibility of this situation ahead of time rather than address it when it happens. The early childhood professional can show empathy for a parent who has feelings about her child's separation behaviors. At the same time, this professional can help the parent understand that it is harder on the child when they come to distrust the parent than it is to express their feelings about separation openly.

Of course, when a child has been in early care and education programs from a young age, he may be quite used to separation, although the first day of kindergarten or first grade may be a bigger one than he is used to. It may be a new setting with new regulations. The group's size may be larger, and having parents in the classroom on the first day isn't as feasible as in programs for younger children.

WHAT TEACHERS CAN DO

- Reassure parents that the child is in good hands.
- Demonstrate acceptance of any upset feelings—both the child's and the parent's. It helps if they can both see that their upset doesn't upset you, too.
- Help parents see that their child's separation anxiety is quite common and nothing to worry about. Indeed, it shows attachment, and that's a good thing. Some parents may take protesting behavior that's an expression of separation anxiety as bad manners. Assure them that you don't see it that way.

Good-byes the first day can be hard. Accept the child's feelings, and try pairing him up with another child. Notice how this teacher is down at eye level with the children when she talks to them.

- If the parent is allowed to and chooses to stay in the classroom to help the child separate gently, suggest that the parent let the child decide when the parent can leave. Although this doesn't always work, it gives the child a sense of self-confidence when it does.
- Pair a new child with another child. Pair the parent with another, more experienced parent.
- Allow "transition objects," something special from home that the child finds comfort in when the separation issues get her down.

A story about starting kindergarten: Nicky was born prematurely, got a rocky start in life, and was medically fragile for the first two years of his life. He had experience in two different early care and education settings before starting kindergarten. Each time he began a new program, his parent remained until he was comfortable staying by himself. Kindergarten was a big step after preschool, though, and Nicky started worrying. Before school started, he attended a parent meeting with his mother. When the teacher announced that the children would stay in the classroom with the aide while the parents took a tour of the school grounds, Nicky grabbed his mother's hand and wouldn't let go. He was the only child that day who got the school grounds tour with the parents. The mother talked to the teacher when the meeting was over to tell her that she always stayed with Nicky in school until he felt comfortable when entering a new program. The teacher was very clear when she said in a firm voice, "No parents in the classroom the first day." Both Nicky and his mother were worried about the first day. They had a talk. His mother explained that this new school had new rules, and even though neither of them liked the one about no parents in the classroom, that's just the way it was. "So what are you going to do?" she asked him. He thought about it for awhile and then said, "I'll go under the table." Once he had a strategy, he felt a lot braver. The first day came, and he let go of his mother's hand and walked straight into the classroom. After the session, she picked him up and was glad to see a big smile on his face. "How did it go?" she asked. "Well," he said. "I did just what I said. I went under the table. Then a girl said, 'Teacher, there's a boy under the table.' So I came out." That's all he ever said about it, but apparently, the strategy worked! The second day, he came up with a new strategy. He wore his Superman tee shirt.

In the "Daily Guidelines" section in this parent handbook, there are some ideas and also some specific instructions under a subsection called "Bringing Your Child."

DAILY GUIDELINES

→ **Bringing Your Child**

It is important to help your child make the transition from home to school. If a staff member has not greeted your child, take your child to one of the teachers. State licensing requires that teachers greet children and their parents and assess the health of the child before the parent leaves.

A few things to remember:

1. You may bring your child ten minutes before the block begins. This gives some time for greeting the teacher, looking around the school with your child, and walking to your class.

2. Sign your child in on the daily sign-in sheet when you arrive. You must use a complete signature.

3. Pin your child's nametag on and assist in hanging up his or her coat.

4. Let teachers know any information that will help them as they work with your child (lack of sleep, change in daily schedule, new medicine, et cetera).

Leaving with Your Child

1. Sign your child out when you pick him/her up. Only persons listed on the Emergency Card may pick up a child. The parent of record must inform the staff verbally and give written permission if someone else is picking-up the child. The person picking-up must check-in with the Children's Center Office and present photo identification before the child can be released.

2. Leave your child's nametag in the place designated by your child's teacher.

3. Check your child's cubby for treasures waiting to go home.

4. Take home wet clothes.

5. If your child has worn DVC extra clothing home, please clean and return it the next day you attend school.

6. CHECK YOUR PARENT MAILBOX. PLEASE READ AND RESPOND TO ANY MEMOS OR NOTICES.

MAINTAINING HOME LANGUAGE

WHAT TEACHERS NEED TO KNOW

There are many misconceptions about children who arrive in school or other early childhood programs with a home language that is different from English. Because these children may be perceived as language deficient or potential candidates for having a language delay, it is important that everyone recognize and appreciate the development these children have made in their own language, regardless of their current proficiency in English. The benefits of preserving home language, and encouraging the child's continued development in it, are many. Adding English to what they already know encourages bilingualism, which is a worthy goal for a number of reasons. (Charmian, 2007). It's important for teachers not to consider bilingualism as a problem but rather as a blessing.

Language and culture are vitally linked. Families use language to pass on their culture to their children and teach them how to grow up and remain members of the particular group or groups to which the family belongs. Thus, language also plays an important role in identity formation. One big issue children have as they grow up is discovering where they belong. Those children who lose their home language also lose important connections to their family and their people.

Neither language nor culture is taught in formal lessons. Rather, both are learned during interactions through which children read the expectations of those around them. Some of these informal "lessons" related to culture may be embedded in language, and some may not.

What is a child's *home language*? Home language can be broadly or narrowly defined. A narrow way of looking at home language is whether dictionaries and grammar books exist to give the language standards. A more useful way for early childhood educators to look at home language is as the language that is spoken in the child's home.

When the great "Ebonics debate" arose in California a few years ago, it was argued across the United States whether teachers should accept the way that some African American children speak. Certainly, it may feel different to support a child when the family speaks Standard English (or, as it is sometimes called, *Status English*) from supporting an Ebonics-speaking child. Or consider two families who both speak Spanish. One speaks Standard Spanish, and the other speaks what some label as "Spanglish." Both Ebonics and the dialects used by children from Spanish-speaking backgrounds are regarded as inferior by some who speak Standard English or Standard Spanish. But it's important to remember that when it comes to language, culture, family ties, and issues of identity, acceptance of the family and their language, whatever it is, makes a difference to the child's self-esteem, which can support learning and development.

When teachers disapprove of the home language, it is important for them to understand that some children pick up messages, spoken or not, that cause them to give up their home language in favor of English. That's a subtractive approach to English language learning. An additive approach is much better. When children learn Standard English as well as continue to develop in their home language, they become bilingual, which has a decided advantage to the child, the family, the community, and the nation. Bilinguals feel at home with their family and also out in the English-speaking world!

Nobody is asking teachers to learn to speak all the languages that may show up in their classrooms. Of course, they aren't going to be required to learn what they may consider a substandard dialect, but there are compelling reasons not to look down on children whose families speak such a dialect. There are also compelling reasons to bring family or community members into the classroom or program if the school or program has no other adults who speak the language of the family.

   Of course, all children in the United States must eventually learn to speak English and to use it in powerful ways. Maintaining home language is a way to support English language learners. If done well, the child can end up bilingual and bicultural, which would be a great educational goal for *all* children in this country—including those from families whose home language is English.

WHAT TEACHERS CAN DO

- Encourage families to work with you to maintain the home language in their children. Share with those families the fact that in this country, historically, the average immigrant family faced the loss of their home language in three generations. Today, it's often only one generation, as children begin to feel ashamed and sometimes make the decision on their own to turn their backs on their parents' and grandparents' language.

- Understand that some families and communities struggle to maintain their home language. Find them and support them in that struggle. Get them together with families that are so concerned with their children learning English that they don't face the risks of losing the home language. If they hear stories of adults who found they couldn't go home and belong there once they lost the language of their family, or hear stories about discipline problems when children and adults no longer share the same language, they may be motivated to work with you to maintain the home language in their children.

- Use the terms *additive bilingualism* with families, and discuss the advantages of being bilingual (see Yoshida, 2008).

- Consider children's emotional state as they are acquiring English, and make their emotional well-being a primary goal.

- Find ways to bring each child's home language into the classroom or center. Children's emotional well-being can be supported by hearing their own language when not at home. Getting families involved can help. Volunteers can also help. Community centers, social groups, and religious groups can be sources of volunteers for the classroom or center.

- Look for books and other materials in the children's home language. Bring in other media as well, such as recorded music from their culture. Live music is even better. Be sure the environment reflects the language and culture of every family in the classroom or center. (See Strategy 4, Creating an Antibias Environment.)

- Language, learning, and thinking are tied together. Encourage children to use their strongest language to help them think through something or solve a problem.

- Become an advocate for bilingualism, and work with others to change unfair English- only assessment practices.

- Be careful to avoid mislabeling those learning English as having disabilities or language delays.

- Don't be fooled by the myth that children pick up a second language in no time at all. It takes years to develop to full academic competence in one's own language; thus, English learners may "pick up" conversational abilities. But having the full range of linguistic competence won't happen any more rapidly than language acquisition in monolingual children will. And of course, if children continue to develop those competencies in their home language and learn English competencies as well, they will eventually become truly bilingual.

- Find resources and support for yourself so that you can do what can be a hard job! Nobody ever said teaching was easy—rewarding, yes, but easy, no!

40 EASING CHILDREN THROUGH TRANSITIONS

WHAT TEACHERS NEED TO KNOW

One of the hardest parts of parenting is keeping up with children moving from one stage to another. The most dramatic moves come in the first two years, but moving from one stage to the next is a continual process throughout childhood and, indeed, throughout life. Behaviors change as children move to the next stage, and parents may see these new behaviors as problems rather than as an indication of greater maturity. Here's where effective education of parents can come in handy. Parents can learn about new approaches they can take that match those of the new stage. Most parents don't take child development courses, so that's a perfect topic for parent education, especially when parents find it helpful. Articles to read, discussion groups, even lectures and videos are gratefully received by families who are facing a new stage with which they aren't familiar.

Moving from stage to stage is one kind of transition. Moving from one classroom to another, or from one program to another, is a kind of transition that sometimes coincides with a developmental change and sometimes not. In a program that tries hard to be developmentally appropriate, very young children may face many transitions if each new stage means a new classroom with a new teacher. When you consider the issue of relationships—child relating to teacher or caregiver as well as parents relating to new adults at each developmental stage—the constant transitioning can be very unsettling. Something called *looping*, where teacher stays with the class or group for several years, is an answer to the problem of continually severed relationships.

No matter what, there always comes a time when children and their parents have to move on. So let's look at some strategies for helping parents help their children to make transitions, whether from one stage to another, from one room to another, or from one program to another.

WHAT TEACHERS CAN DO

- Take your position as a parent educator seriously. Just as you respond to the care and education of children as individuals, so should you respond to parents as individuals. Some parents are new at parenting, and they may be real beginners without ever having been around children before. They are most likely eager to know more, especially if they perceive you as a resource and not a threat—as someone who can give them ideas, but who will not criticize them. Other parents may be much more experienced at parenting. They can also be resources to parents who need skills, information, and support.

- There are many ways to facilitate learning. Just as early childhood professionals pay attention to the different learning styles of children, so they can pay attention to those of parents and other family members. What works best? It could be articles tucked into the parent's mailbox in response to questions asked; discussions around a topic that a parent or group of parents show interest in; a lending library, with a variety of materials on lots of subjects related to parenting; a list of suggested readings; observations followed by discussion; videos; and pairing experienced parents with inexperienced ones. These are just a few ideas for how to match teaching approaches and resources to individual learning styles.

- Transitions that are not stage related should be slow and not occur too often. Some children suffer greatly even with a small transition, like that from one activity to another. They resist change—even little changes. They don't like new things. Other children are less reluctant, but transitions create some stress in almost all children. (See Strategy 38 for more ideas about how to ease transitions.)

- Remember that with every transition children make, the family is also affected. Moving on is felt by everybody.
- If the child care program lacks what can be called *continuity of care*, consider the advantage of a family child care home as an early care and education setting when it comes to lowering the number of transitions. Some family child care providers have several children from the same family and may stay connected with the family for years. Children come as newborn babies into a family child care home and may be there until they outgrow early care and education! In some cases, the child grows up, has children of his own, and sends those children to the same provider he went to in his early years. Talk about long-term relationships and continuity of care!

A story: One infant-toddler program decided to institute a continuity-of-care system where babies stayed with the same caregivers until they were old enough to move to preschool, which was housed in the same building. The caregivers stayed with the group even though the environment changed as the babies outgrew the room they started out in. The first time around, nobody knew exactly how this would work, and some were doubtful that it would. There was some resistance on the part of the care-givers, because they were used to a certain age group and didn't think they would like working with older or younger children. But that turned out not to be a problem once they got connected to the babies. They really enjoyed "moving up with them" and seeing more of the developmental sequence unfold. By the time the first group was almost old enough to transition to preschool and leave the infant-toddler staff behind, there was some concern about the separation process. After being with the same caregiver for so long, wouldn't they suffer when they said good-bye? The surprise was that the children did great. They were excited about becoming preschoolers, and the transition was slow enough that they got used to the preschool room and teachers before the final move came. The new world and people in it were so interesting and exciting to them that the separation was a gentle one. Even the caregivers found letting go easy, because they felt the children were ready to move on and they knew they would continue to see them. They just wouldn't be their caregivers any more. The other surprise was that the group who suffered separation anxieties was the parents! They worried a good deal about the new teacher and the new program. They just didn't want to let go of the people they had grown to know and trust!

41 BRINGING NATURE INTO CHILDREN'S LIVES

WHAT TEACHERS NEED TO KNOW

With childhood obesity rates rising, it becomes clearer and clearer that something is wrong with the lifestyle of many American children. It's easy to see the roots of this problem when you look to the beginning of life for the average American baby. Strapped into various devices, which reduces their ability to exercise, babies spend most of their waking and all of their sleeping hours indoors in recycled air. They are set up for a sedentary, indoor lifestyle.

Comparing the average American baby's life and health with the babies studied for more than 60 years in a residential nursery in Budapest, Hungary, you see quite a contrast. The nursery, called The Pikler Institute after its founder, Dr. Emmi Pikler, brought science together with some old-fashioned ideas about fresh air, exercise, and freedom to explore both in and out of doors. Babies and young children in the Institute not only play outdoors every day except in the most extreme weather, they also nap outside—from birth on (Gonzalez-Mena, 2004).

Part of this old-fashioned idea is that children should be free to move and explore, which at the Pikler Institute they learn starting in infancy. Instead of being strapped into baby carriers, swings, and strollers or being sat up in high chairs, the babies at the Pikler Institute move naturally, unencumbered by modern baby equipment. As a result, they gain movement skills, balance, and above all, motivation to learn. They grow into active preschoolers who see themselves as competent learners who don't need adults gushing over them praising every little thing they accomplish or offering rewards for learning. They are natural learners, eager to discover, find out how things work, and gain knowledge of everything around them and beyond.

Put children who have that kind of early education into a classroom where they are required to sit and memorize disembodied facts or repeat answers to questions on flash cards for long periods and you can see that either they will cause problems or they will come to take on a less active lifestyle. That inactive lifestyle is definitely a trend, as outside pressures make teachers teach in ways they may not necessarily agree with. Added to this is the fact that in some schools, recess is an endangered species, because it is thought to cut into learning time.

Richard Louv (2008a, b) is trying hard to reverse one of these trends, which he calls the *denatured childhood*. He is a champion for exploration and free play in natural surroundings, which some children never in their lives have a chance to do. He cites studies that show the time spent indoors in front of the television and computer relates to growing obesity in children (and in adults, too).

Free, unstructured play is important to children's mental, physical, and emotional health. Free play that takes place in natural surroundings increases cognitive flexibility, emotional capacity, critical thinking, problem solving, creative use of imagination, self-esteem, and self-discipline. It makes children smarter, more cooperative, more energetic, happier, and healthier. Playing in natural settings is valuable, because nature is a highly complex system and is a lot bigger than all of us. Children can find more to do in natural settings than in most other settings, because nature has a good many of what play theorists call *loose parts*. "In any environment, both the degree of inventiveness and creativity, and the possibility of discovery, are directly proportional to the number and kind of variables in it" (Simon Nicholson, quoted in Gies, 2008, p. 26).

Spending time in a natural environment encourages children to take reasonable risks, which is an important part of growing up. The child who has always been in a risk-free environment, under adult control at all times, or both has little experience in judging which risks he or she can handle and

Getting children outside in natural settings gives them exercise, fresh air, and hopefully, an appreciation or at least an acquaintance with the natural world.

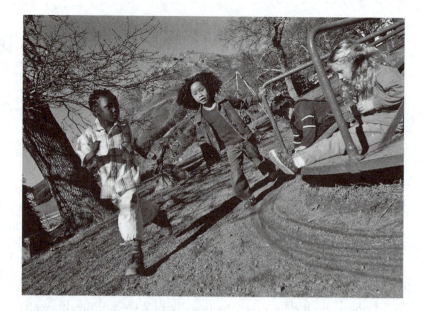

Bringing things like this chrysalis inside to study helps children understand and appreciate nature.

which ones are worth taking. Learning what one is physically capable of is an essential childhood task, and it is learned in particular environments where there are opportunities for taking reasonable risks. According to Gies (2008), a study at the University of Illinois has found that contact with nature and the accompanying risk-takings involved can even reduce attention deficit disorder.

WHAT TEACHERS CAN DO

- Observe your daily schedule, and calculate the amount of time children spend in free and unstructured play that is not part of an adult-directed game or activity. If the constraints work against expanding free play, or if there is no chance at all for free play during the school day, get together with the parents, and figure out how to expand that time outside of school, especially if it tends to be limited.
- Become more aware of nature-deficit disorder, and together with the parents, figure out what to do about it. A good start would be to get back to nature yourself (if you need to) and so provide a model for the parents and children alike. Your enthusiasm can be contagious.

- Bring nature into the classroom in ways that children can get involved with in a hands-on way. See if you can find some parents to partner with you in this attempt.
- Become an advocate for stopping the de-naturizing of your community and for restoring nature where possible. Some forward-looking schools are tearing up sections of asphalt in the playground and planting gardens.
- Become an advocate (and bring parents along with you) for putting nature study into the curriculum if it not is already there. Teach natural history in developmentally appropriate ways, depending on the age of the child.

42 ADDRESSING OBESITY WITH NUTRITION

WHAT TEACHERS NEED TO KNOW

More American children are overweight than ever before. Why? One reason is lack of exercise (See Strategies 41 and 43.) Another reason is an unhealthy diet. According to Michael Pollan in his book *In Defense of Food*, most people's diet consists of highly processed, food-like products rather than real food. Those products contain vast amounts of refined wheat and amazing amounts of sugars and corn syrups—even those that don't taste sweet. Though vitamins and minerals are added, the end product is still far less nutritious than the original, unprocessed food substance. Meat is full of hormones designed to make animals fat and tasty, but when meat is consumed and those same hormones go into human bodies, they may be adding to weight problems.

One mother with a girl in child care complained to the teachers and the directors about the daily menu, which she felt was sadly lacking in proper nutrition. Because the program depended on government funding and therefore had to follow government guidelines, they couldn't do much to change things. Here's a place where advocacy can help, though the various food lobbies that want to keep the status quo in Washington, D.C., are powerful.

By the time children get to kindergarten and the early grades, their food tastes and what they are accustomed to are pretty well set. That's why parental involvement and education are so important in the early years. Once teachers and parents get together and explore nutritious food choices, both groups can learn from each other. Of course, cultural differences may be great, but that can be an advantage if families are still eating the diets of their ancestors. It seems that the simple, natural diets of yesteryear were much healthier—without all the additives and innovations of modern food processing. But of course, there are lots of pressures to take on the common diets of today, which include a heavy dose of fast food eaten in cars and on the run as well as prepared food, whether frozen in ready-to-heat containers or in boxes off the grocery store shelves.

WHAT TEACHERS CAN DO

- Help parents understand the value of fresh food over processed food products, and work to provide more fresh food if you or the program is responsible for what the children eat while away from home.
- Set examples of healthy eating habits. Look for nutritious snacks to serve at parent meetings. Get parents to contribute ideas and food.
- Bring in cooking experts to demonstrate how to make delicious food out of healthy ingredients.
- Have meetings to exchange ideas with families on nutritional issues.
- Grow food, if possible, and involve the children. There's nothing like pulling out a carrot you helped grow and then eating it for snack. Make parents part of your gardening activity, and encourage parents to take the idea home and try it themselves.
- Get children in small groups to cook in class, if such a thing is possible. Involve parents in this so that they can do the same at home. A number of academic lessons come out of one cooking activity. Early literacy is one lesson when you use individual recipe cards. If you're teaching children who are old enough to read, the cards can contain words. If you're working with younger children, pictures will work—and the children are still getting "reading lessons" when they see a

Whoever packed this lunch box seems to know about the health benefits of fresh fruit.

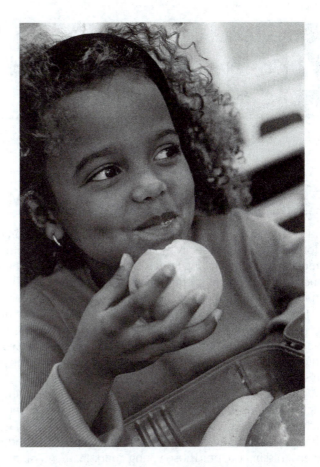

series of picture symbols and find the meaning in them. Children get math lessons as they measure ingredients—two tablespoons of this and half a teaspoon of that. And if children are working in groups, it also becomes a socialization activity.

A story about working with parents around nutrition: A woman who worked with low-income parents decided to have a series of parent meetings around nutritional issues. She brought in an expert chef who did cooking demonstrations, after which the parents in attendance ate the delicious dishes they had learned to prepare. The chef introduced ingredients that were inexpensive and easy to come by, but not well known by, the families. The ingredients were also highly nutritious. These new dishes caught on, and the parents loved the cooking lessons. Quite a different approach than giving a lecture on nutrition and making parents feel guilty about what they were feeding their children!

43 DEALING WITH MEDIA ISSUES

WHAT TEACHERS NEED TO KNOW

One electronic media issue is the health concern that can come from the sedentary lifestyle that television and computer use promote. Another issue related to health is the formation of eating habits that come along with watching television—the excess calories and the lack of nutrition in the snacks consumed, both of which can be influenced by advertising. The effect that watching violence on television and in computer games has on young children is another negative against electronic media.

Jane Healy, an educational psychologist and author of three books about early childhood learning, is a strong advocate for helping teachers and parents take a good look at the time young children spend with screens instead of out in the real, physical world. We don't need research to tell us that addiction to screens is widespread—and growing—in the population across the whole age range. We can see it everywhere we go.

These addictions can start in infancy as babies are propped up in front of the television screen to watch programs with images and sounds designed especially for them. Add to that how parents or teachers are anxious to prepare children for the future by getting them started on computers. The huge issue here is what are young children who spend a good deal of time looking at or interacting with screens missing out on? Those young children are missing out on what earlier generations did in childhood during their free time—running around outdoors and playing with other children. A lot of them were playing in natural surroundings.

Nobody ever proved that children have to be sitting down to learn. Young children are active learners, and they need plenty of chances to move, explore, and play freely, which they may not be getting at home. They also need concrete experiences as part of their learning. Because of using screens as both entertainment and learning tools, children today are doing much more sitting and watching than any generation in history. No wonder obesity is a growing problem.

According to Healy (2008), "Time spent with computers in the early years not only subtracts from important developmental tasks but may also entrench bad learning habits, leading to poor motivation and even symptoms of learning disability" (p. 75). That's a strong statement!

No one has shown that computers in preschool contribute to children's learning, development, health, or well-being, though computers and software are being developed and marketed to families with young children and to early childhood teachers. It's up to families and teachers to be wise about what they buy for children.

Learning should be in a physical and social context, not coming through disembodied screens. Children learn best when they have personal interactions with adults and other children. As Healy (2008) puts it, "The brain does its important work in a context of relaxed exploration guided primarily by the child and supported by helpful and emotionally responsive but not overly intrusive adults" (p. 76).

In those situations, children are also learning to focus their attention instead of flitting from one thing to another. Electronic media, with its bells and whistles, pop-ups, graphics, and other distractions, works against a steady stream of attention.

Along with other early childhood experts, Healy sees age 7 as the appropriate time to begin using computers to help children learn. She says that computer learning for young children, even those at age 7, should be backed up with manipulative activities away from the screen. For many educators and psychologists, age 7 is a developmental milestone—children are getting their second set of teeth,

Addiction to television can start in infancy and continue into the adult years.

and their brains are less tied to the here and now of the concrete world. However, they still learn concretely; thus, manipulative materials that they can touch, hold, and move around are still important.

Plenty has been written about young children viewing violent programming and the danger of commercials turning even toddlers into consumers. Certainly, parents should be involved in discussions about the effect of the amount of violence children are seeing on screens at home, and parents should do what they can to eliminate or at least minimize it. That's where parents as advocates can make a difference in what is shown during prime time, when children have easy access to such media.

Children's experiences in natural settings are greatly reduced when they spend a good deal of their days and evenings in front of screens. It doesn't work to just show them nature programs as a substitute. There are no fresh air, exercise, and sensory experiences that go along with watching nature programs. Furthermore, these programs set up expectations so that when children do get outdoors to encounter nature in person, they expect to see things happen like they have seen on television—birds hatching from eggs or bull moose fighting. With those kinds of expectations, children may find being out in nature boring, because things don't happen so fast as compared to nature on screens. It takes patience and observation skills to study nature; watching films doesn't necessarily promote those skills (except in the photographers who make the movies).

WHAT TEACHERS CAN DO

- Work with parents to help their children live a healthier lifestyle by monitoring electronic media and endeavoring to reduce the negative effects that come from overusing some kinds of media.
- If you aren't now using computers but are being pressured to do so, help those who are applying the pressure to understand that starting children too early can create much bigger problems than starting them too late.
- Do make some important decisions before you go into computers. Don't spend money unless you already have all the other materials you need that are developmentally appropriate. Don't skimp on those to get computers.
- If you do already have or are going to get computers, set them up so that computer use is a social experience. Let children work together and talk while they are working.
- Prepare yourself by observing how children use computers, and if you see problems, start thinking how to solve them.
- Get training in using computers with young children.
- Research and make sure you are buying developmentally appropriate software.

- Be clear about what you want children to learn from the computer, and look for software that accomplishes your goal. Don't be dazzled by programs that don't do what you want.
- If you are using DVDs or television, make sure what you show is developmentally appropriate. Eliminate commercials if you can. Limit the time children spend sitting and watching. Be sure you have plenty of active and interactive learning experiences going on.
- Discuss issues around electronic media with parents and other family members. Share ideas. Discuss how to solve the problems that can arise.

MAINTAINING STABILITY DURING DIVORCE

 ## WHAT TEACHERS NEED TO KNOW

Special attention is needed for children and families who are going through a divorce, which is a major transition for all the family members and may involve angry feelings and inappropriate behavior by the two people getting divorced. A breakup often involves financial stress as well as a move from the original residence. A lower standard of living for the children may also be a result. This period may bring feelings of loss, because one parent is no longer as much a part of the children's lives. Sometimes the siblings are split up. The original family no longer exists in the same way. There may be a long, unsettled period in which life is not predictable and a sense of security is disrupted. The rocky period usually starts before the actual divorce occurs as parents go through a period (long or short) of conflict.

WHAT TEACHERS CAN DO

- Though you can't do anything about the tensions being felt at home, you can help parents deal with their children's feelings and resulting behaviors, which may include fears, sleep disturbance, fussing, and whining. Sometimes children regress—go back to an earlier time in their life and pick up old behaviors that they had shed long ago, such as bed-wetting or thumb sucking. The ordinarily easy-to-get-along-with child may become demanding, defiant, or disobedient. The usually secure child may become dependent and show separation anxiety. In recess or playtime, you may notice less positive interaction, more aggression, and perhaps, less involvement as the usually active child becomes more of an observer. Older children may look sad, have difficulty focusing, and show fear, anxiety, or anger.
- Sometimes children may conclude that the divorce was their fault. It's important they understand that this is not true and that they are not to be blamed.
- Of course, parents have their own feelings, and although you are not a therapist, you can still offer them support. You can't meet their needs, but you can listen to them if they feel like talking. On the other hand, they may not feel like talking. They may be so upset that they turn away and become less interactive with the teacher or caregiver. Understanding and empathy are the best response to changes in parental attitudes and behavior during this difficult period.

Even a divorce can have some light spots. This child may be indicating that rain can result in rainbows.

- Community resources are available for families in stress. Know what they are, and make information available to the parents. You can't be all things to all people, but you can point family members toward the help they might need for counseling. Parents Without Partners can be a support for them, too. Have contact information available.
- Make available books about divorce—for both children and adults.
- Be very clear about who is authorized to pick up the children and who is not.
- Know that this period will pass. Be kind, gentle, and understanding.
- Examine your own attitudes and feelings about divorce. Become aware of any stereotypes you may have about families who are undergoing this transition or about the consequences for children. It is different for each family and for each person in the family. The process of the divorce may make for difficult times and correspondingly difficult behavior, but don't decide that you already know the long-term effects on the children. Many of the ideas about negative outcomes do not hold true. Children are not necessarily worse off because their parents divorce, nor are they worse off living in single-parent families than in two-parent families. There are many myths and misconceptions about children of divorced parents. Certainly, if the parents were miserable together, that situation has a negative effect on the children, which can go away once the split comes.

45 COPING WITH A DEATH IN THE FAMILY

WHAT TEACHERS NEED TO KNOW

A death in the family can be a traumatic event for everybody—and especially for a child. The death of the parent who is the main caregiver can be devastating, because not only is there a sense of loss but also tremendous feelings of insecurity as the child asks, consciously or unconsciously, "Who will take care of me now?" Death can shake a child to his or her very core and affect the child's development and sense of self. A good deal of support is needed—both for the child and for the family members. Teachers aren't therapists, but there are some things they can do to help the child and the family through what is bound to be a difficult period.

Many factors enter into how the death affects the child. A slow death, with the child supported through the dying process, is very different from, say, a sudden and violent death. Of course, any death in the family is likely to leave lasting effects as a child goes through a grieving process, but a sudden, violent death—especially one witnessed by the child—can add serious trauma to the grieving.

Not only does the child suffer acute loss with the death of a parent, the child is likely to experience disruption of his or her whole life. Living situations may change, and there's bound to be some interruption of the daily routines. The accompanying stress can affect not only the child's behavior but also his or her development. According to Alicia Lieberman and her coauthors (2003), "When an attachment figure dies, the child loses intimate patterns of interaction that organize key developmental domains and constitute the building blocks for the child's sense of self" (p. 10). If there is a surviving parent, that person may be unavailable to give emotional support to the child because of his or her own grieving and adjusting to the changing life circumstances.

The nature of the death also influences the reactions. Some deaths can represent social stigmas—dying from AIDS, for example, or being murdered while in prison or committing suicide. Those deaths are quite different from parents who die in the line of duty, such as members of the military, police officers, or firefighters. Their survivors may have conflicting emotions. Seeing loved ones as heroes deserving gratitude can mix pride with grief. But survivors can also experience resentment that the loved one chose service over family duties and died for that choice.

WHAT TEACHERS CAN DO

- Anticipate that there may be some behavioral changes in the child whose parent died. It helps to understand that these behaviors and the feelings behind them are mourning responses. Be prepared for crying, anger, fears, anxiety, frustration, increased aggression, and possible regression.
- Keep things as familiar as possible. Teachers and other early care and education professionals can provide a dependable, stable environment with predictable routines, which may be a contrast to what the child is getting at home.
- Give the child emotional support through all the stages of grieving: 1) hoping the lost parent will return, and then finally giving up that hope; 2) integrating the memories of the parent into an ongoing sense of self; and 3) turning to another attachment figure to find emotional bonds (Lieberman, Compton, Van Horn, & Ippen, 2003, p. 7).
- Recognize that the children's behaviors, such as protesting, emotional withdrawal, anger, and aggression that are aimed at you are grief responses. Don't take them personally.

- Allow children to play out their feelings. Not only does the grieving child need opportunities to express feelings through words or play, the other children may also be feeling anxious.
- Be aware that holidays, when many programs have children make cards and presents for their parents, may be hard on the child in mourning. Consider expanding the activities to include a wide variety of significant others in each child's life. Be especially available to the bereaved child during these activities.
- Recognize the grief in the other adults in the family, and do what you can to support them emotionally.
- Pay attention to your own feelings. Death affects everyone, and you are no exception. You have your own issues and history. Separate those from the present circumstance in this family with this child.
- If appropriate, get the surviving family members connected to other parents in the program so that they can get additional support.
- Don't try to be a therapist. If the child or family needs therapy, help them find a referral. (See Strategy 46, Finding Community Resources and Making Referrals.)

46 FINDING COMMUNITY RESOURCES AND MAKING REFERRALS

WHAT TEACHERS NEED TO KNOW

When schools and other early care and education programs focus on the sharing of information and resources, everybody benefits. It isn't just the professionals who have information—families have their own resources that they can share with staff and other families. A sharing spirit makes the difference between a program in which the staff gives and the families receive and one in which the giving and receiving are reciprocal. That program becomes a community. (See Strategy 14 about creating a community.) The problem is that this doesn't happen easily. The professionals are busy with the children, and when it comes to resources, they are lucky if they have a list to give out.

A huge question arises with low-income and homeless families. How can teachers and caregivers create partnerships with parents and expect them to be part of their children's care and education if the family's basic needs are not being met? Economic welfare is a vital requirement for food, clothing, and shelter. Families who lack the ability to provide for the basic needs of their children come to schools and early care and education programs in significant numbers. According to the Children's Defense Fund (2004), "More than 12 million children are poor and millions more live in struggling families with incomes just above the official poverty line" (p. 1). That's one out of six children.

Many of the children in schools and early care and education programs come from single-parent families, and some of those children or family members have disabilities and other kinds of challenges. According to Turnbull and Turnbull (2001), "Those households headed by a single parent who has a child with a developmental disability have the lowest income of any household type" (p. 217).

We won't be able to solve a family's economic problems with the strategies in this chapter, but an understanding about family support services can help teachers, caregivers, and providers direct families to the community resources that can help them. From its early beginning, Head Start recognized the importance of connecting the community to their programs and the families to the community. This federally funded program has long served as a model for other programs.

Here is some information about supports for low-income families. The federal program designed to provide economic help is called TANF (Temporary Assistance for Needy Families). Social Security provides income assistance for low-income families who have children with disabilities under SSI (Supplemental Security Income). Medicaid is a federal program providing medical assistance for low-income people. Even though they are underfunded, these three programs can begin to address some of the economic and medical needs. Some states have programs that help to fill in where federal programs have proved to be insufficient.

WHAT TEACHERS CAN DO

- Ethel Seiderman (2003), who founded an organization called the Family Services Project, said, "Community building based on caring relationships encourages optimal availability and use of resources. Accessing resources doesn't happen in a vacuum" (p. 360). She offers some strategies for becoming an early care and education program that emphasizes family support services:
  ○ Revise your own image of your program to include being part of the economic and human service infrastructure of the community. Network with community leaders.

Schools and child care programs are natural meeting places "to bring together the needs of children and families and the community resources that they may need to access" (Seiderman, 2003, p. 358).

- ○ Become known, and make your voice heard in your community, including attending school board meetings. Become a speaker at social, business, and professional groups in the community.
- ○ Partner with various community organizations so that together, you are stronger.
- • Turnbull and Turnbull (2001) offer some strategies that early childhood professionals can use in collaboration to improve economic situations for the families they serve:
  - ○ Make sure that the director, teachers, caregivers, or other staff members know about the potential resources that might help families. Those include TANF, the federal Earned Income Tax Credit, state income and other tax credits, food stamps, child support enforcement income, plus child-related resources, such as health benefits—Medicaid or the state child health insurance program—and child care subsidies.
  - ○ When a program or class includes children with identified or suspected disabilities, make sure someone on the staff knows about early intervention or special education services.
  - ○ Team up with other community organizations, such as domestic violence, mental health, and substance abuse agencies, to address prevention and treatment issues for vulnerable families.
  - ○ Increase advocacy along with parents and other groups at both state and local levels to do the following (see also Strategy 13 on advocacy):
    - ■ Improve the availability of high-quality child care and education that is responsive to family needs.
    - ■ Promote economic and security supports for families while working on a shared agenda that is focused on families with the most severe barriers to meeting their economic needs.

WORKING WITH PARENTS WHO CONSTANTLY COMPLAIN

WHAT TEACHERS NEED TO KNOW

One parent is always in the principal's office with a new criticism or complaint. She used to talk to the teacher but he got tired of it, so the teacher got really busy when she was around. Now she goes to the principal. This is not an uncommon situation.

Before her child was old enough to go to school, he was in child care. This mother's behavior there was the same. She was always complaining to the staff and went to the director on a regular basis. Staff meetings were regularly taken up with this one mother's complaints. Why all these complaints?

Only when you understand what's going on with this parent can you determine what to do about it. It helps to think about how parents, usually mothers, are responsible for the well-being of their young children, which includes even the most personal aspects of their daily care. When all of that is out of the parents' hands, such as in child care or school, they may feel frustrated that they can't control or, to some extent, even know how it is being done. This can weigh heavily on parents when they have the responsibility but are not in charge because they have to delegate it.

Lynet Uttal (2002) made an ethnographic study of mothers who had children in child care arrangements. and she found, among other things, that the responsibility for choosing care and education programs for their children was left up to mothers, even if fathers or other family members were part of the picture. With responsibility comes the potential for error. The mothers wanted very much to believe that their children were getting high-quality care, but they were worried a good deal that perhaps they had made a bad choice and their children were not in the best situation. They exhibited ambivalence in most cases, and it centered on how to monitor and ensure the quality of their arrangements. Worries about safety were high on the list. Programming and staffing were also concerns. These mothers were constantly wondering about things like what was the relationship like between their child and the professional? What kind of care was their child getting? What if their child cried and nobody paid attention? What caused that bruise on the child's leg? How was the child being disciplined? Or was there no discipline? Those questions weighed heavily on the minds of the women Lynet Uttal interviewed.

Of course, every article in the newspaper about suspected abuse in a family child care home or center intensifies all the worries. Who is watching out for the children is a question parents have to ask when their children are in homes and institutions where they can't monitor them very well.

In Uttal's study, how comfortable mothers were about their children's out-of-home experience depended on the relationships they had with their children's care and education professionals. Uttal made it clear that relationships really matter!

The mother in the story that opened this chapter doesn't seem to have had much of a relationship with the staff in child care or, later, with the teacher in her child's school. It's easy to say it is her own fault, but is it? Whose responsibility is it to build the relationship? In a world where parents may feel like guests at best and intruders or spies at worst in their children's school or other care and education settings, it is up to the professionals to help them feel otherwise by working on building a relationship with each one.

So let's look back at the mother who always criticizes and complains. Maybe behind the complaints are worries and frustrations. Maybe she has ambivalent feelings about her child being away from her. Maybe she feels guilty. Are her criticisms and complaints a way of making her feel like she is taking charge? Fulfilling her responsibilities? Maybe this parent is feeling like the responsibility for her child is out of her hands and she wants to have more involvement in it. Only she doesn't know how to get involved except to be critical of what is going on. In that case, give her more options to be part of things.

A completely different explanation might be that maybe this parent feels she doesn't get enough attention. Maybe the only way that anybody listens to her is when she complains. She's like the child who is ignored until he misbehaves. You can't just keep ignoring the child—or the parent, either. They need attention, and they are getting it in a way that works. You have to show them that other ways work, too. Give her recognition when she is not complaining. It may not be easy, but just as we can work with children by giving them the attention they need at appropriate times, we can do the same with adults.

WHAT TEACHERS CAN DO

- Try to understand what it must be like to be in this mother's position.
- Work on building a relationship with her by initiating contact instead of sending her away when she initiates it. Get to know her. Find a way to spend some time with her when you're not so busy with the children. If you begin to relate to one another, her complaining may ease up.
- Take her seriously, and try to make her feel at home in the program.
- Try to get her involved in helping out.
- Introduce her to some other parents.
- Discuss with the principal or director what else can be done.
- Get other staff members involved.

48 WORKING WITH PARENTS WHO APPEAR HOSTILE

WHAT TEACHERS NEED TO KNOW

Let's look at a parent who is often angry, aggressive, and seems to harbor deep hostility. This is a parent who presents real challenges to many early childhood professionals. Those of us who work with young children may have a tendency to be nice and want others to be nice as well. That's not true of all of us, but it is an impression one gets when in the field for very long. Teachers, caregivers, and staff who like "nice" may give up on working with what they consider to be a hostile parent. Interestingly enough, most teachers don't give up on children as readily as they do parents. In fact, some teachers energize themselves to take on a challenging child while they want to turn their back on an angry parent. Some even want to run away and hide! Worse, some give up on all parents because of a few difficult experiences. (See Strategy 7, Removing Barriers to Partnerships.)

WHAT TEACHERS CAN DO

- Avoid labeling parents or anybody else. Labels can get in the way of your ability to work with others.
- Separate your feelings from the parents' feelings, like you do with children. Notice when defensive or aggressive feelings arise in you. Getting angry in the face of anger is not usually an effective response if this is a person with whom you are trying to establish a relationship. An experienced professional learns to step aside from a child's anger and not take it personally. Most can acknowledge the feelings without getting caught up in them. Just as we do that for children, we can learn to do that for adults.
- Try to accept the feelings and understand them if you can. Don't overanalyze; you aren't a therapist. But do realize that, for example, a parent's strong feelings may relate to genuine concern for her child. A parent may lack skills for communicating concerns. Instead of being assertive about what's bothering her, she may use aggression instead. Sometimes behavior comes out the opposite of what the feeling is. People with low self-esteem act conceited, people who feel powerless can become pushy, and people who are afraid may exhibit anger instead.
- Recognize that strong feelings are not usually about whatever triggers them but have deeper roots. Fear and grief may well show up as anger toward someone who has nothing to do with what makes the angry person afraid or puts him in mourning.
- Your job is to remain calm and work to open up communication by becoming aware of what blocks communication, such as:
  - ○ Defensive responses
  - ○ Arguing
  - ○ Criticizing
  - ○ Distracting
- Practice what has long been called *active listening*, a time-honored strategy used by early childhood educators. Thomas Gordon (2000) named this strategy in his book *Parent Effectiveness Training*. Originally designed for use with children, active listening also works well with adults. It is a way of acknowledging feelings so that the other person realizes you are accepting rather than

criticizing them—or trying to make them go away. Put into nonjudgmental words what you perceive. The trick is to hit the nail on the head. If you say, "You seem irritated," and the parent is furious, then you missed the mark. But if he or she corrects you, then at least you've got a start on communication.

- Realize that the time and effort you put into working with an angry parent may result in your meeting up with the nice person underneath the angry cover.

49 TALKING WITH PARENTS ABOUT BEHAVIOR CHANGES

WHAT TEACHERS NEED TO KNOW

Todd is having a hard time lately in class. He used to be easygoing and able to get along with everybody, but lately, he has changed a good deal. He refuses to comply with the rules. He argues with everybody, including the teacher. He always seems tired, and sometimes he just sits and stares off into space. He has always been a happy, active child, so the change in Todd's behavior has his teacher worried. She wonders if this is a stage he is going through. Maybe something is going on at home. The teacher decides to talk to his mother.

Talking to his mother is a fine idea, but if the purpose of the conversation is to ask about what is going on at home that would explain the change in Todd's behavior, the teacher should reconsider. This approach to understanding child behavior is so common in early care and education that most professionals don't think twice about it.

Jim Greenman (2003) was an advocate for not prying into a family's private life in the name of understanding the child better. He said, "Respect for parents demands that, unless the situation is one of abuse or neglect, the parents control what information they wish to share" (p. 317). Greenman questioned the idea that teachers have any more right to know about what goes on in the family than the family has a right to know about teachers' private lives. If a teacher is going through a divorce, should a notice go home to the parents to watch for changes in the children's behavior because their teacher is so stressed out? What if the parents were told to be understanding with their children and give them extra attention because of what is going on at school?

If you can see that a child is under stress, do you really need to know why? Will you treat him differently if you know the roots of his stress? Why not just support him and give him what he needs regardless of what is going on at home? Greenman suggests giving flexibility, warmth, and nurturing to the child who is under stress. If Todd, for instance, wants to talk about how he feels, the teacher can listen. And if Todd's parents come to the teacher and want to share what's going on, that's very different from the teacher asking.

The following are some ideas about how to relate to parents when you see a change of behavior in their children.

WHAT TEACHERS CAN DO

- Be a good observer. Be clear about what the changes are and under what circumstances they occur.
- Respond to the child's behavior in ways that help him relax, if possible. Let him know he has your support and understanding. Do what you can to meet his needs.
- If you see that he's feeling pressure while in the classroom, do what you can to ease the pressure.
- Set and keep limits for the child, but do so in calm and gentle ways. See if you can make things easier for the child at school. Meet his needs as best as you can. If you determine that he is feeling pressure in the classroom, ease off.
- If you ask the parent to talk with you about the situation at school, be prepared to share your own observations and what you are doing to respond. Report what has worked and what hasn't. Listen to any suggestions the parent might have about how to work with the behaviors.
- Make sure your observations are reported in nonjudgmental terms. Describe behavior without putting value judgments on it.

- Respect the parent's right to privacy. Don't ask what is going on at home. If the parent wants to share with you what is happening, keep this information confidential. Offer your support, and use your best listening skills. Don't offer advice.
- If the parent hasn't already given you suggestions for how to work with her child in school, ask her, and then listen to her ideas. Give them a try. They just might make a difference.
- You can do all of the above without needing to know if the parents are getting a divorce, the father got laid off or is in jail, there's a new baby in the family (although the parents or the child are likely to share that news with you voluntarily), or grandma just died and grandpa came to live with them. Any one of those situations could cause a change in behavior. You can work with the change without knowing the reason it came about.

50 REFERRING FAMILIES FOR ABUSE OR NEGLECT

WHAT TEACHERS NEED TO KNOW

Abuse and neglect are heartbreaking conditions for anyone to face, yet everyday, children who are victims of such treatment come into classrooms and early care and education programs along with their families. Legal definitions of abuse and neglect differ by state, but in general, abuse is characterized by mistreatment that either results in physical harm or is likely to harm the child. Physical abuse includes spanking only if the child is bruised or injured in some other way. Sexual abuse includes any form of sexual conduct in which children are used to provide sexual gratification for the perpetrator. Also included as sexual abuse are any forms of sexual exploitation, including child pornography. Emotional abuse is harder to see, but it relates to rejection, isolation, and corruption of a child. Terrorizing a child is a form of emotional abuse. And under certain circumstances, even ignoring a child can be considered emotional abuse. Emotional abuse includes such widely ranging examples as allowing a child to engage in criminal activity, inattention to a child's need for psychological help, verbal abuse, and exposing a child to domestic violence. Neglect falls into a different category of abuse and is characterized by refusal to meet basic needs, including affection and attention or withholding health care.

It may seem as if abuse and neglect happen only among low-income families, but that's not true. Abuse and neglect happen at all levels of society, although maltreatment occurs more often to children who have disabilities. There are some risk factors that should be considered. Certainly, poverty can cause stress, and stress can cause abuse. Isolation of the family from others can be another risk factor. The coping skills of the family and lack of anger management can contribute to the possibility of abuse. Health issues in the family can result in neglect of a child. Characteristics of the actual child can be a factor in abuse and neglect as well. When several of these factors work together, the family is more vulnerable. Knowing the families you work with may help you direct some to support services and prevent abuse before it happens.

Anyone who works with young children is a mandated reporter—by law, that person must report any suspected abuse or neglect. You don't have to prove it, just suspect it. If you suspect abuse, be sure you have your facts straight, and have some kind of grounds for your suspicions. Don't do anything with the family yourself. Your school or program may have a reporting procedure—an authority to go to as the second step, such as the director, the principal, or the school social worker. Finally, call your local child protection agency to report.

If families have been referred to your program after having been identified by authorities as having maltreated their children, it is your job to work with them. You may have feelings about their children and what they have been through. Nevertheless, you need to approach these families with the same openness, acceptance, and respect with which you approach any other family. It may be a challenge to do so, but that's what is needed. In the long run, everybody benefits.

WHAT TEACHERS CAN DO

- Becoming aware of your own feelings and attitudes is important. You may feel angry with a parent for an injury she caused to her child, but your job is to get to know her and work to understand, respect, and support her.

- Build a trusting relationship with all parents, including those who have been referred for abuse or neglect. It may be especially difficult because you are a mandated reporter and the parents know that. They may not see you as being "on their side." It is important that you work as hard to relate to them as you do to other parents or family members. One way to show that you are trustworthy is to keep confidentiality. Do not talk about a family to others.
- Don't assume that children who have been abused and neglected no longer feel close to their parent(s). Attachment usually holds up even in extremely abusive circumstances. Be very careful that you do not say anything negative to children about their parents. Show them that you support both them and their parents.
- Help prevent abuse by doing the following:
  - Providing support when needed, or referring to outside sources of support. If parents have been referred to your program because of their problems with abuse or neglect, it is likely that they already are connected with a support group. For other families under stress, keep up to date on community resource information. Know the numbers for parental hotlines, family support centers, crisis centers, parent support groups, Parents Anonymous, and counseling and parental education programs. Preventing abuse and neglect is a much better approach than addressing abuse and neglect after they occur.
  - Offering ideas for increasing parenting skills, such as guidance using problem-solving strategies and approaches rather than physical punishment.
  - Modeling nonviolent and nonaggressive approaches to conflict resolution in the classroom with the children.
  - Working with children who lack social skills to improve them. Some child behaviors put them at risk for being abused in families that have other risk factors as well.

This excerpt from a preschool parent handbook is a fairly standard statement about the legal mandate that early care and education professionals have to report suspected child abuse. In some programs, families enrolling their children are required to sign a statement that they understand suspected child abuse will be reported to the authorities.

15

Menus

Monthly menus are posted in the kitchen area in both centers and on the bulletin boards near the entry doors. Menus are available to parents upon request.

Food Allergies

Be sure to notify us of any food allergies. Food allergies are listed on the front of the child's nametag and on lists posted in the children's eating areas and on the refrigerators.

Minor modifications can be made to many of our menus to meet the needs of children with allergies (e.g. burritos with no cheese or white flour tortillas instead of whole wheat). Parents with children with extreme food allergies should ask for menus to determine any day when their child is unable to eat what is being served. On that day, the parent needs to bring a main course item for the child. It should be marked and given to a staff member.

Other Allergies

Pets and regular outside play are parts of our daily curriculum. If your child has an extreme allergy, please let us know.

Child Abuse

All employees of the DVC Developmental Children's Center are mandated to report suspected instances of child abuse, mental suffering or endangerment of the emotional well being of children that they become aware of in their professional capacity, or within the scope of their employment.

We want to work with all of the adults whether they are parents, staff or students associated with our Center to keep children safe and healthy. Additional helpful information is available from the Family Stress Center in Concord (925/827-0212) or the Contra Costa County Child Abuse Prevention Council (925/946-9961).

References

Akbar, N. (1985). *The community of self*. Tallahassee, FL: Mind Productions.

American Academy of Family Physicians. (2003). Definition of Family. Retrieved January 15, 2009, from http://www.aafp.org/online/en/home/policy/policies/f/familydefinitionof.html

American Psychological Association Online. (2004). *What is sexual orientation?* Retrieved February 10, 2009 from http://www.apa.org/pubinfo/answers.html

Baker, A. C., & Manfredi-Petitt, L. A. (1998). *Circle of love: Relationships between parents, providers and children in family child care*. St. Paul, MN: Redleaf Press.

Baker, A. C., & Manfredi-Petitt, L. A. (2004). *Relationships, the heart of quality care: Creating community among adults in early care settings*. Washington, D.C.: National Association for the Education of Young Children.

Balaban, N. (2006). *Everyday goodbyes: Starting school and early care, a guide to the separation process*. New York: Teachers College Press.

Ballenger, C. (1992, Summer). Because you like us: The language of control. *Harvard Educational Review, 62*(2), 199–208.

Barrera, I., & Corso, R. (2003). *Skilled Dialogue*. Baltimore, MD: Brookes.

Basso, K. (2007). To give up on words: Silence in Western Apache culture. In L. Monaghan & J. E. Goodman (Eds.), *A cultural approach to interpersonal communication* (pp. 77–87). Malden, MA: Blackwell.

Bennett, T. (2007). *Mapping family resources and support: Spotlight on young children and families*. Washington, D.C.: National Association for the Education of Young Children.

Bhavnagri, N., & Gonzalez-Mena, J. (1997, Fall). The cultural context of caregiving. *Childhood Education, 74*(1), 2–8.

Bisson, J. (2002). *Celebrate: An antibias guide to enjoying holidays in early childhood programs*. St. Paul, MN: Redleaf Press.

Bisson, J. (2008). Holiday lessons learned in an early childhood classroom. In A. Pelo (Ed.), *Rethinking early childhood education* (pp. 165–170), Milwaukee, WI: Rethinking Schools.

Bloom, P. J., Eisenberg, P., & Eisenberg, E. (2003, Spring/Summer). Reshaping early childhood programs to be more family responsive. *America's Family Support Magazine*, 36–38.

Brand, S. (1996, January). Making parent involvement a reality: Helping teachers develop partnerships with parents. *Young Children, 51*(2), 76–81.

Brault, L., & Brault, T. (2005). *Children with challenging behavior*. Phoenix, AZ: CPG Publishing.

Brault, L. M. V. (2007). *Making inclusion work: Strategies to promote belonging for children with special needs in child care settings*. Sacramento, CA: California Department of Education.

Bravo, E. (2008). It's all of our business: What fighting for family-friendly policies could mean for early childhood educators. In A. Pelo (Ed.), *Rethinking early childhood education* (pp. 197–200). Milwaukee WI: Rethinking Schools.

Bredekamp, S. (2003). Resolving contradictions between cultural practices. In C. Copple (Ed.), *A world of difference*. Washington, D.C.: National Association for the Education of Young Children.

Bredekamp, S., & Copple, C. (1997). *Developmentally appropriate practice in early childhood programs* (2nd ed.). Washington, D.C.: National Association for the Education of Young Children.

Bruno, H. E. (2005, September). At the end of the day: Policies, procedures and practices to ensure smooth transitions. *Exchange, 16*, 66–69.

Caldwell, B. (2003). Advocacy is everybody's business. In B. Neugebauer & R. Neugebauer (Eds.), *The art of leadership* (pp. 46–48). Redmond, WA: Exchange Press.

Cannella, G. S. (1997). *Deconstructing early childhood education: Social justice and revolution*. New York: Peter Lang.

Carlson, V. J., & Hawwood, R. L. (1999–2000). Understanding and negotiating cultural differences concerning early developmental competence: The six raisin solution. *Zero to Three, 20*(3), 19–23.

Carroll, K. 2007. *A guide to great field trips*. Chicago: Zephyr.

Casper, V. (2003). Very young children in lesbian- and gay-headed families: Moving beyond acceptance. *Zero to Three, 23*(3), 18–26.

Chang, H. N., Muckelroy, A., & Pulido-Tobiassen, D. (1996). *Looking in, looking out: Redefining child care and education in a diverse society*. Oakland, CA: California Tomorrow.

Chao, R. (1994). Beyond parental control and author-itarian parenting style: Understanding Chinese parenting through the cultural notion of training. *Child Development, 65,* 1111–1119.

Charmian, K. (2007). Childhood bilingualism: Research on infancy through school age. *Literacy, 41*(2), 110–111.

Children's Defense Fund. (2004). *The state of America's children.* Washington, D.C.

Chodron, P. (2000). *When things fall apart.* Boston: Shambhala.

Clay, J. (1990). Working with lesbian and gay parents and their children. *Young Children, 45*(3), 31–35.

Clay, J. (2004). Creating safe, just places to learn for children of lesbian and gay parents: The NAEYC Code of Ethics in action. *Young Children, 59*(6), 34–38.

Cohen, B. (2008, July/August). Communicating with parents about food allergies. *Exchange, 182,* 61–65.

Colabucci, L., & Conley, M. D. (2008). What makes a family: Representations of adoption in children's literature. In T. Turner-Vorbeck & M. M. Marsh (Eds.), *Other kinds of families: Embracing diversity in schools* (pp. 139–160). New York: Teachers College Press.

Copple, C., & Bredekamp, S. (2009) *Developmentally appropriate practice in early childhood programs serving children birth through age 8* (3rd ed.). Washington, D.C.: National Association for the Education of Young Children.

Council on Interracial Books for Children. (2008). 10 quick ways to analyze children's books for racism and sexism. In A. Pelo (Ed.), *Rethinking early childhood education* (pp. 211–214), Milwaukee, WI: Rethinking Schools.

Covey, S. R. (2002). Foreword. In K. Patterson, J. Grenny, R. McMillan, & A. Switzler, *Crucial conversations* (pp. xi–xv). New York: McGraw-Hill.

Dowhey, M. (2008). Heather's moms god married. In A. Pelo (Ed.), *Rethinking early childhood education* (pp. 177–179). Milwaukee, WI: Rethinking Schools.

Curtis, D., & Carter, M. (2003). *Designs for living and learning.* St. Paul, MN: Redleaf Press.

Daniel, J. E. (1998, November). A modern mother's place is wherever her children are: Facilitating infant and toddler mothers' transitions in child care. *Young Children, 53*(6), 4–12.

Daper, L., & Duffy, B. (2001). Working with parents. In G. Pugh (Ed.), *Contemporary issues in the early years: Working collaboratively for children.* London: Paul Chapman Publishing.

Darragh, J. (2008, July/August). Access and inclusion: Ensuring engagement in EC environments. *Exchange, 182,* 20–23.

David, M., & Appell, G. (2001 [1973, 1996]). *Loczy: An unusual approach to mothering.* Translated from *Loczy ou le maternage insolite,* by Jean Marie Clark; revised translation by Judit Falk. Budapest: Association Pikler-Loczy for Young Children.

DeLoache, J., & Gottlieb, A. (2000). *A world of babies: Imagined childcare guides for seven societies.* New York: Cambridge University Press.

Delpit, L. (1995). *Other people's children: Cultural conflict in the classroom.* New York: The New Press.

Derman-Sparks, L. (2008). Why an antibias curriculum? In A. Pelo (Ed.), *Rethinking early childhood education* (pp. 7–12). Milwaukee, WI: Rethinking School.

Derman-Sparks, L., & the Antibias Curriculum Task Force. (1989). *The antibias curriculum: Tools for empowering young children.* Washington, D.C.: National Association for the Education of Young Children.

DeWeese-Parkinson, C. (2008). Talking the talk: Integrating indigenous languages into a head start classroom. In A. Pelo (Ed.), *Rethinking early childhood education* (pp. 175–176). Milwaukee, WI: Rethinking Schools.

Diffily, D. (2001, Summer). Family meetings: Teachers and families build relationships. *Dimensions of Early Childhood,* 5–9.

DiNatale, L. (2002, September). Developing high-quality family involvement programs in early childhood settings. *Young Children, 57*(5), 90–95.

Dombro, A. L., Colker, J., & Dodge, D. T. (1999). *The creative curriculum for infants and toddlers* (Rev. ed.). Washington, D.C.: Teaching Strategies.

Dreikurs, R., & Stolz, V. (1990). *Children the Challenge.* New York: Penguin.

Edelman, M. W. (2003, October 19). Children in America: A report card. Interview in *Parade Magazine,* p. 13.

Eggers-Pierola, C. (2005). *Connections and commitments: A Latino-based framework for early childhood educators.* Portsmouth, NH: Heinemann.

Eisaguirre, L. (2007). *Stop pissing me off!* Cincinnati, OH: Adams Media.

Epstein, J. L. (2001). *School, family, and community partnerships: Preparing educators and improving schools.* Boulder, CO: Westview.

Fasoli, L., & Gonzalez-Mena, J. (1997, March). Let's be real: Authenticity in child care. *Exchange, 150,* 35–40.

Fernandez, M. T., & Marfo, K. (2005). Enhancing infant-toddler adjustment during transitions to care. *Zero to Three, 26,* 41–48.

Fitzgerald, Damien. (2004). *Parent partnership in the early years.* London: Continuum.

Galinsky, E. (1998, March). Parents and teacher-caregivers: Sources of tension, sources of support. *Young Children, 43*(3), 4–12.

Garner, A. (2004). *Families like mine: Children of gay parents tell it like it is.* New York: HarperCollins Publishers.

Gartrell, D. (2004). *The power of guidance.* Washington, D.C.: National Association for the Education of Young Children.

Geelen, A. (2009, January). Investigating nature in New Zealand. *Wonder: Tawa Montessori School strives for "hundred-acre wood" in the backyard, 1*(2), 1–3.

Gelnaw, A., Brickley, M., Marsh, H., & Ryan, D. (2004). *Opening doors: Lesbian and gay parents and schools.* Washington, D.C.: Family Pride Coalition.

Gestwicki, C. (2004). *Home, school, and community relations: A guide to working with parents.* Albany, NY: Thompson Delmar.

Gies, E. (2008, Fall/Winter) Playing it smart! *Land and People, 20*(2), 24–31.

Gonzalez-Mena, J. (1997, July). Cross cultural conferences. *Exchange, 116,* 55–58.

Gonzalez-Mena, J. (1997, September). Understanding the parent's perspective: Independence or interdependence? *Exchange, 117,* 61–64.

Gonzalez-Mena, J. (1999, July). Dialogue to understanding across cultures. *Exchange, 128,* 6–8.

Gonzalez-Mena, J. (2002, January/February). Personal power: Creating new realities. *Child Care Information Exchange, 143,* 59–62.

Gonzalez-Mena, J. (2004, September). What can an orphanage teach us? Lessons from Budapest. *Young Children, 60*(5), 26–29.

Gonzalez-Mena, J. (2007, May/June). Thinking about thinking: How can I get inside your head? *Exchange, 175,* 50–52.

Gonzalez-Mena, J. (2008a). *Diversity in early care and education: Honoring differences* (5th ed.). New York: McGraw-Hill.

Gonzalez-Mena, J. (2008b). *Foundations of early childhood education in a diverse society* (4th ed.). New York: McGraw-Hill.

Gonzalez-Mena, J. (2009). *Child, family and community: Family-centered early care and education* (5th ed.). Upper Saddle River, NJ: Merrill/Prentice Hall.

Gonzalez-Mena, J., & Bernhard, J. K. (1998, Summer). Out-of-home care of infants and toddlers: A call for cultural and linguistic continuity. *Interaction, 12*(2), 14–15.

Gonzalez-Mena, J., & Eyer, D. (2009). *Infants, toddlers, and caregivers,* (8th ed). New York: McGraw-Hill.

Gonzalez-Mena, J., & Shareef, I. (2005, November). Discussing diverse perspectives on guidance. *Young Children, 60*(6), 34–38.

Gonzalez-Mena, J., & Stonehouse, A. (2003, July/August). High-maintenance parent or parent partner? Working with a parent's concern. *Child Care Information Exchange,* 16–18.

Gonzalez-Mena, J., & Stonehouse, A. (2008). *Making links: A collaborative approach to planning and practice in early childhood programs* (American ed.). New York: Teachers College Press.

Gordon, T. (2000). *Parent effectiveness training.* New York: Three Rivers Press.

Greenman, J. (1998, November/December). Parent partnerships: What they don't teach you can hurt. *Child Care Information Exchange,* 78–82.

Greenman, J. (2003). Places for childhood include parents too. In B. Neugebauer & R. Neugebauer (Eds.), *The art of leadership.* Redmond, WA: Exchange Press.

Greenman, J., & Stonehouse, A. (1996). *Prime times: A handbook for excellence in infant and toddler care.* St. Paul, MN: Redleaf Press.

Greenwood, P. M., & Cocking, R. R. (1994). *Cross-cultural roots of minority child development.* Hillsdale, NJ: Erlbaum.

Hale-Benson, J. (1986). *Black children: Their roots, culture and learning styles.* Baltimore, MD: Johns Hopkins University Press.

Hall, E. T. (1981). *Beyond culture.* Garden City, NY: Anchor Press/Doubleday.

Harkness, S., & Super, C. M. (Eds.). (1996). *Parents' cultural belief systems.* New York: Guilford Press.

Harwood, R. L., Miller, J. G., & Irizarry, N. L. (1995). *Culture and attachment: Perceptions of the child in context.* New York: Guilford Press.

Haynes-Lawrence, D. (2009, January/February). Crisis nurseries: Emergency services for children and families in need. *Exchange, 185,* 16–20.

Healy, J. (2008). Cybertots: Technology and the preschool child. In A. Pelo (Ed.), *Rethinking early childhood education* (pp. 75–84). Milwaukee, WI: Rethinking Schools.

Hernandez, L., & Smith, C. J. (2009, January/February). Disarming cantankerous people: Coping with difficult personalities in the ECE work settings. *Exchange, 185,* 12–14.

hooks, b. (2003). *Rock my soul: Black people and self-esteem.* New York: Atria.

Hudson, R. A. (2007). Speech communities. In L. Monaghan & Goodman, J. E. (Eds.), *A cultural approach to interpersonal communication* (pp. 212–217). Malden, MA: Blackwell.

Jacobson, T. (2003). *Confronting our discomfort: Clearing the way for antibias in early childhood.* Portsmouth, NH: Heinemann.

Jones, E. (2007). *Teaching adults revisited: Active learning for early childhood educators.* Washington, D.C.: National Association for the Education of Young Children.

Jones, E., & Cooper, R. (2006). *Playing to get smart.* New York: Teachers College Press.

Kagiticibasi, C. (1996). *Family and human development across cultures.* Mahwah, N.J.: Erlbaum.

Kaiser, B., & Rasminsky, J. S. (2003). *Challenging behavior in young children: Understanding, preventing, and responding effectively.* Boston: Allyn and Bacon.

Katz, L. (1977). *Talks with teachers: Reflections on early childhood education.* Washington, D.C.:

National Association for the Education of Young Children.

Katz, L. (1996). Child development knowledge and teacher preparation: Confronting assumptions. *Early Childhood Research Quarterly, 11*(2), 135–146.

Keeler, R. (2009, January/February). A spring playscape project: Building a tree circle. *Exchange, 185,* 70–71.

Keyser, J. (2001). Creating partnerships with families: Problem-solving through communication. *Child Care Information Exchange, 138,* 4–7.

Kitayama, S., Markus, H., & Matsumoto. (1995). Culture, self, and emotion: A cultural perspective on "self-conscious" emotions. In J. P. Tangeny & K. W. Fischer (Eds.), *Self-conscious emotions: The psychology of shame, guilt, embarrassment, and pride.* New York: Guilford Press.

Kreidler, W. J., & Whitall, S. (2003). Resolving conflict. In C. Copple (Ed.), *A world of difference: Readings on teaching children in a diverse society* (pp. 52–56). Washington, D.C.: National Association for the Education of Young Children.

Kroeger, J. (2008). Doing the difficult: Schools and lesbian, gay, bisexual, transgendered, and queer families. In T. Turner-Vorbeck & M. M. Marsh (Eds.), *Other kinds of families: Embracing diversity in schools* (pp. 121–138). New York: Teachers College Press.

Lakey, J. (1997, May). Teachers and parents define diversity in an Oregon preschool cooperative—Democracy at work. *Young Children, 52*(4), 20–26.

Lally, J. R. (1995, November). The impact of child care policies and practices on infant-toddler identity formation. *Young Children,* 51(1), 58–67.

Lane, M., & Signer, S. (1990). *A guide to creating partnerships with parents.* Sacramento, CA: California Department of Education and WestEd.

Lee, L. (2004). *Stronger together: Family support and early childhood education.* San Rafael, CA: Parent Services Project.

Lee, L., & Seiderman, E. (1998). *Families matter: The Parent Services Project,* Cambridge, MA: Harvard Family Research Project.

Lesser, L. K., Burt, T., & Glenaw, A. (2005). *Making room in the circle: Lesbian, gay, bisexual and transgender families in early childhood settings.* San Rafael, CA: Parent Services Project.

Levine, J. A. (1993a). *Getting men involved: Strategies for early childhood programs.* New York: Scholastic.

Levine, J. A. (1993b). Involving fathers in Head Start: A framework for public policy and program development. *Families in Society, 74*(1), 4–19.

Lewis, C. C. (1995). *Educating hearts and minds: Reflections on Japanese preschool and elementary education.* New York: Cambridge University Press.

Lewis, E. G. (1996). What Mother? What Father? *Young Children, 51*(3), 27–30.

Lieberman, A. (1995). Concerns of immigrant families. In P. Mangione (Ed.), *A guide to culturally sensitive care* (pp. 28–37). Sacramento, CA: California Department of Education and WestEd.

Lieberman, A. F., Compton, N. C., Van Horn, P., & Ippen, C. G. (2003). *Losing a parent to death in the early years.* Washington D.C.: Zero to Three.

Lin, C. Y., & Fu, V. (1990). A comparison of child-rearing practices among Chinese, immigrant Chinese, and Caucasian-American parents. *Child Development, 61,* 429–433.

Link, G., & Beggs, M., with Seiderman, E. (1997). *Serving families.* Fairfax, CA: Parent Services Project.

Logue, M. E., Shelton, H. Cronkite, D., & Austin, J. (2007, March). Family ties: Strengthening partnerships with families through toddlers' stories. *Young Children, 62*(2), 85–87.

Lopez, E. J., Salas, L., & Flores, J. P. (2005, November). Hispanic preschool children: What about assessment and intervention? *Young Children, 60*(6), 48–54.

Louv, R. (2008). Don't know much bout natural history: Education as a barrier to nature. In A. Pelo (Ed.), *Rethinking early childhood education* (pp. 133–136). Milwaukee WI: Rethinking Schools.

Louv, R. (2008). *Last child in the woods: Saving our children from nature-deficit disorder.* Chapel Hill, NC: Algonquin Books of Chapel Hill.

Lubeck, S. (1996). Deconstructing "child development knowledge" and "teacher preparation." *Early Childhood Research Quarterly, 11*(2), 147–168.

Maltz, D. N., & Borker, R. A. (2007). A cultural approach to male-female miscommunication. In L. Monaghan & J. E. Goodman (Eds.), *A cultural approach to interpersonal communication* (pp. 77–87). Malden, MA: Blackwell.

Mangione, P. (Ed.). (1995). *A guide to culturally sensitive care.* Sacramento, CA: California Department of Education and WestEd.

Marks, I. (2008). Wards of wisdom: foster youth on a path toward postsecondary education. In T. Turner-Vorbeck & M. M. Marsh (Eds.), *Other kinds of families: Embracing diversity in schools* (pp. 81–102). New York: Teachers College Press.

Martin, J. (2009, January/February). Using the principles of intentional teaching to communicate effectively with parents. *Exchange, 185,* 53–56.

Maschinot, B. (2008). *The changing face of the United States: The influence of culture on child development.* Washington, D.C.: Zero to Three.

Meisels, S. J., & Atkins-Burnett, S. (2005). *Developmental screening in early childhood.* Washington, D.C.: National Association for the Education of Young Children.

Miller, K. (2005). *Simple transitions for infants and toddlers.* Beltsville, MD: Gryphon House.

Modigliani, K. (1997). *Parents speak about child care.* Boston: Wheelock College Family Child Care Project.

Moerman, M. (2007). Talking culture: Ethnography and conversation analysis. In L. Monaghan & J. E. Goodman (Eds.), *A cultural approach to interpersonal communication* (pp. 119–127). Malden, MA: Blackwell.

Monaghan, L. (2007). Conversations: The link between words and the world. In L. Monaghan & J. E. Goodman (Eds.), *A cultural approach to interpersonal communication* (pp. 145–149). Malden, MA: Blackwell.

Monaghan, L., & Goodman, J. E. (Eds.). (2007). *A cultural approach to interpersonal communication.* Malden, MA: Blackwell.

Negri-Pool, L. L. (2008). Welcoming Kalenna: Making our students feel at home. In A. Pelo (Ed.), *Rethinking early childhood education* (pp. 161–169). Milwaukee, WI: Rethinking Schools.

Neubauer, B. (2009, July/August). Celebrating Mother Nature. *Exchange, 182,* 18–19.

New, R. S. (1999, March). Here, we call it "drop off and pickup": Transition to child care, American style. *Young Children, 54*(2), 34–35.

North, M., Durekas, T., Siegel, B., & Sisbarro, A. (2009, January/February). The ins and outs of transporting children on field trips. *Exchange, 185,* 84–85.

Nyman, S. I. (2003). Mentoring advocates in the context of early childhood education. In B. Neugebauer & R. Neugebauer (Eds.), *The art of leadership* (pp. 54–57). Redmond, WA: Exchange Press.

Olson, M. (2007, March). Strengthening families: Community strategies that work. *Young Children, 62*(2), 26–32.

Palmer, P. (1997). *The courage to teach.* San Francisco: Jossey-Bass.

Parent Services Project (PSP). (2001). *Working together for children and families* [Brochure]. San Rafael, CA.

Parlakian, R. (2001). *The power of question: Building quality relationships with families* [Brochure]. Washington, D.C.: Zero to Three.

Pelo, A. (2008) A pedagogy for ecology. In A. Pelo (Ed.), *Rethinking early childhood education* (pp. 123–130). Milwaukee, WI: Rethinking Schools.

Pelo, A. (2008). Bringing the lives of lesbian and gay people into our programs. In A. Pelo (Ed.), *Rethinking early childhood education* (pp. 180–182). Milwaukee, WI: Rethinking Schools.

Pelo, A. (Ed.). (2008). *Rethinking early childhood education.* Milwaukee WI: Rethinking Schools.

Perry, B (2006). Applying principles of neurodevelopment to clinical work with maltreated and traumatized children. In. N. B. Webb (Ed). *Working with traumatized youth in child welfare* New York: Guilford Press.

Petrie, S., & Owen, S. (2005). Authentic relationships in group care for infants and toddlers: Resources for infant Educarers (RIE) principles into practice. London: Jessica Kingsley Publishers.

Phillips, C., & Cooper, R. (1992). Cultural dimensions of feeding relationships. *Zero to Three, 12*(6), 10–13.

Phillips, C. B. (1995). Culture, a process that empowers. In P. Mangione (Ed.), *A guide to culturally sensitive care* (pp. 2–9). Sacramento, CA: California Department of Education and WestEd.

Pollan, M. (2008). *In Defense of Food* New York: Penguin Press.

Pope, J., & Seiderman, E. (2001, Winter). The child-care connection. *Family Support, 19*(4), 24–35.

Prieto, H. V. (2009, January). One language, two languages, three languages … more? *Young Children, 64*(1), 52–53.

Ramirez, A. Y. (2008). Immigrant families and schools: The need for a better relationship. In T. Turner-Vorbeck & M. M. Marsh (Eds.), *Other kinds of families: Embracing diversity in schools* (pp. 28–45). New York: Teachers College Press

Ramirez, C. (2008). Strawberry Fields Forever? An early childhood teacher draws on her past to teach children of migrant farmworkers. In A. Pelo (Ed.), *Rethinking early childhood education* (pp. 171–174). Milwaukee, WI: Rethinking Schools.

Rosenkoetter, S., & Knapp-Philo, J. (Eds.). (2006). *Learning to read the world: Language and literacy in the first three years* Washington, D.C.: Zero to Three.

Ratekin, C., & Bess, G. (2003). Making the partnership stronger—Working with a board of directors. In B. Neugebauer & R. Neugebauer (Eds.), *The art of leadership* (pp. 110–113). Redmond, WA: Exchange Press.

Rieger, L. (2008). A welcoming tone in the classroom: Developing the potential of diverse students and their families. In T. Turner-Vorbeck & M. M. Marsh (Eds.), *Other kinds of families: Embracing diversity in schools* (pp. 64–79). New York: Teachers College Press.

Rishel, T. J. (2008). From the Principal's Desk: Making the school environment more inclusive. In T. Turner-Vorbeck & M. M. Marsh (Eds.), *Other kinds of families: embracing diversity in schools* (pp. 46–63). New York: Teachers College Press.

Ritter, J. (2007, March). Tips for starting a successful community partnership. *Young Children, 62*(2), 38–40.

Robinson, A., & Stark, D. R. (2002). *Advocates in action: Making a difference for young children.* Washington, D.C.: National Association for the Education of Young Children.

Rogoff, B. (1990). *Apprenticeship in thinking.* New York: Oxford University Press.

Rogoff, B. (2003). *The cultural nature of human development.* New York: Oxford University Press.

Rothstein-Fisch, C. (2003). *Bridging cultures: Teacher education module.* Mahwah, NJ: Erlbaum.

Russell, G. M. (2004). Surviving and thriving in the midst of antigay politics. *The Policy Journal of the Institute for Gay and Lesbian Strategic Studies, 7*(20), 1–7.

Seiderman, E. (1997, January). Parent/staff partnerships. *Child Care Information Exchange, 113,* 47–49.

Seiderman, E. (2003). Putting all the players on the same page: Accessing resources for the child and family. In B. Neugebauer & R. Neugebauer (Eds.), *The art of leadership* (pp. 58–60). Redmond, WA: Exchange Press.

Shonkoff, J., & Phillips, D. (eds.) (2000). *From neurons to neighborhoods: The science of early childhood development.* Washington D. C. National Academy Press

Simons, K. A., & Curtis, P. A. (2007, March). Connecting with communities: Four successful schools. *Young Children, 62*(2), 12–20.

Small, M. (1998). *Our babies, ourselves: How biology and culture shape the way we parent.* New York: Anchor Books.

Sullivan, D. (2003). *Learning to lead.* St. Paul, MN: Redleaf Press.

Tannen, D. (2007). Conversational signals and devices. In L. Monaghan, & J. E. Goodman (Eds.), *A cultural approach to interpersonal communication* (pp. 150–160). Malden, MA: Blackwell.

Thaxton, S. M. (2003). Grandparents as parents: Understanding the issues. In B. Neugebauer & R. Neugebauer (Eds.), *The art of leadership* (pp. 323–325). Redmond, WA: Exchange Press.

Thoennes, T. (2008). Emerging faces of homelessness: Young children, their families, and schooling. In T. Turner-Vorbeck & M. M. Marsh (Eds.), *Other kinds of families: Embracing diversity in schools* (pp. 162–176). New York: Teachers College Press.

Tobaissen, D. P., & Gonzalez-Mena, J. (1998). *A place to begin: Working with parents on issues of diversity.* Oakland, CA: California Tomorrow.

Triandis, H. C. (1989). Cross-cultural studies of individualism and collectivism. *Nebraska Symposium on Motivation, 37,* 43–133.

Turnbull, A., & Turnbull, R. (2001). *Families, professionals, and exceptionality: Collaborating for empowerment* (4th ed.). Upper Saddle River, NJ: Merrill/Prentice Hall.

Turner-Vorbeck, T., & Marsh, M. M. (2008). *Other kinds of families: Embracing diversity in schools* New York, Teachers College Press.

Trumbull, E., Diaz-Meza, R., Hasan, A., & Rothstein-Fisch, C. (2001). *Five-year report of the Bridging Cultures Project: 1996–2000.* San Francisco: WestEd. Retrieved January 28, 2005 from http://www.WestEd.org/BridgingCultures

Trumbull, E., & Farr, B. (2005). *Language and learning: What teachers need to know.* Norwood, MA: Christopher-Gordon.

Unell, B. C., & Wyckoff, J. L. (2000). *The eight seasons of parenthood. How the stages of parenting constantly reshape our adult identities.* New York: Time Books.

Uttal, L. (2002). *Making care work: Employed mothers in the new childcare market.* New Brunswick, NJ: Rutgers University Press.

Whiting, B. B., & Edwards, C. P. (1998). *Children of different worlds: The formation of social behavior.* Cambridge, MA: Harvard University Press.

Wood, K., & Youcha, V. (2009). *The ABC's of the ADA: Your early childhood program guide to the American's with Disabilities Act.* Baltimore: Brookes.

Yoshida, H. (2008, November). The cognitive consequences of early bilingualism. *Zero to Three, 29*(2), 26–30.

Zepeda, M., Gonzalez-Mena, J., Rothstein-Fisch, C., & Trumbull, E. (2006). *Bridging cultures in early care and education: A training module.* Mahwah, NJ: Erlbaum.

Index